PSYCHO-CULTURAL ADJUSTMENT OF FOREIGN STUDENTS AT COLLEGES IN THE UNITED STATES

Charles I. Anemelu (MA, EdD)

Lumen Educational Publications

Copyright © 2019 by Charles Anemelu

All rights reserved. No part of this publication may be reproduced, distributed, or transmitted in any form or by any means, including photocopying, recording, or other electronic or mechanical methods, or by any information storage and retrieval system, without the prior written permission from the copyright owner.

Paperback
ISBN – 10: 0-9980275-3-7
ISBN – 13: 978-0-9980275-3-1

ABSTRACT

The current study is an attempt to examine post-migration psycho-cultural adjustment factors that potentially inhibit foreign- born students' (FBS) adjustment at community colleges (CCs) in the United States. Although much research has been conducted to better understand various aspects of FBSs' adjustment challenges, little attention has been paid to their post-migration psycho-cultural adjustment challenges especially in the community college setting. This study employs both quantitative and qualitative approaches to examine this research problem. The quantitative phase examined the influence of six (three-compound) factors on the major areas of adjustment of FBSs at participating community colleges in the Northeastern US. The qualitative phase explored and identified the influence of those factors on FBSs' adjustment on the community college campus and their possible explanations. Post-migration psycho-cultural variables including identity consciousness and home nostalgia (ICHN); psychological disorientation and cultural inflexibility (PCCI); family attachment and academic maladjustment (FAAM) were almost all relatively implicated in predicting FBSs' maladjustment on campus. One way analysis of variance (ANOVA) revealed statistically significant interactions among certain sub-groups, of the predictor (independent) variables, with certain sub-scales of the criterion (dependent) variables. In addition, following post hoc (Tukey's HSD) tests, interesting differences emerged in the patterns of prediction especially for marital status, year in college, family presence continents of origin, as well as varied age ranges. Gender had no statistical significance. Among others, family attachment and home nostalgia emerged as more salient predictors of FBSs' psycho-cultural adjustment at CCs. Overall, an aggregate of the mixed-method study findings suggests that foreign-born students (FBSs) have moderate to high level of psycho-cultural adjustment challenges at CCs. This study concludes with the consideration that psycho-cultural influences are fairly unique to Asian, African, and South American, Middle Eastern, and surprisingly to European FBSs as well. Implications for administrators, counselors, educators, and policymakers working in the community college settings are discussed.

ACKNOWLEDGEMENTS

Ad Maiorem Dei Gloriam!

Dissertation writing will always remain a unique experience in the academic life of every doctoral program student. I have a beautiful message for the committee members that guided me to this point of penning down my acknowledgements: Having you as a committee has certainly renewed my love and respect for my *alma mater,* Seton Hall University. It has also deepened my personal appreciation and gratitude to God for who I am and whom it is necessary that I strive to improve upon. The summary is: Gratitude.

I am grateful to my first mentor, Dr. Elaine Walker. Permit me to bring to your knowledge that your involvement in this process, at the fullness of time, not only made an exceptionally positive impact but also shone a brilliant light that will endure forever. Certainly, this is neither a forum to applaud your academic genius nor an attempt to publicize your patience, humility and respect for everyone; coupled with your altogether inimitable simplicity. It is simply to thank you for guiding me through this process with the desired experience and trusted expertise.

I am grateful to my second mentor, Dr. Rong Chen. Let me stress how honored I am to have someone like you on my committee till the end of this process. Indeed, among other things, your intelligence, thoroughness, boldness, admirable pertinacity and perspicacity radiated throughout this journey. Please know that the statistical and factor analysis advisement you once provided, beyond your regular office hours and all other sacrifices you made to help in this process, without stint, are gratefully appreciated.

I am grateful to my third mentor, Dr. Gerard Babo. Thank you very much for saying *yes* when you were called upon to help despite your multifarious academic, dissertation and sundry commitments. No doubt, it was really quite providential that you also got involved in the nick of time. Please know how much I appreciate your invaluable help, advice and constructive comments which additionally provided suitable directions for this project. I am also greatly honored to have you on my committee. I do appreciate your uplifting scholarship as well as your generous commitment and willingness to help others grow.

I am also grateful to Dr. Joseph Stetar who handled us in two dissertation classes and with whom I began my proposal writing journey. I wish to let you know that your own contributions in this process are quite memorable and helpful too. I appreciate them.

My further gratitude goes to Dr. Eunyong Kim, who also assisted in our two major proposal dissertation classes. I recall that you were actually the person who gave the first nod that study was doable. Please know that I do appreciate your keen editorial assistance as well as your favorable recommendations at the onset.

I cannot leave this page without being grateful to Dr. Sandra Lee of the Department of Professional Psychology and Family Therapy. She was among those who gave me the first positive nudge to get registered for classes, in the first place, as well as saw me through during my masters' degree program in psychological studies.

As a posthumous acknowledgement and worthy recognition, I am grateful to Msgr. Kevin Hanbury for the unique roles which he played in the course of my journey at Seton Hall University especially in the admissions' process; both for the master's and doctoral program. I am deeply saddened that he is not here today to witness the final stage of my journey in this noble institution. May the good Lord rest your great soul in perfect peace!

I am grateful to all the community colleges that permitted me to work on this project using their institutions as study sites and their foreign-born students as participants. In a special way, I am most grateful to all the foreign- born students who made this research possible by volunteering for both the pilot test and the main study which comprised survey exercises and a focus group session. Please know how much I appreciate your availability and assistance.

I am grateful to the Seton Hall University TLTC personnel, the student assistants along with their colleagues, who unstintingly helped to transcribe my survey data; both for the pilot test and the main study, into the spreadsheet using the excel program. I once imagined how I would have ever been able to do that singlehandedly without you. Thank you and thank you again for being generous to me with your time and talents.

In addition, I would like to acknowledge my appreciation to a few other persons who contributed in one way or the other toward the success of this project. They include: Drs. A. Walker, J. Yasin, S. Pinkerton, V. Anemelu and Mr. C. Ezeogu. I am thankful especially for your helpful suggestions, useful contributions and very considerate editorial assistance.

Special thanks to all those who played encouraging and supportive roles during this arduous journey: Most Rev. Dr. V.M. Okeke, Msgr. Jim Brady, Frs. E. Anarado, A. Vellaramparampil, J. Meagher and L. Lemaitre. Others include: Frank, Mary and Joseph Ocello, Retrd. Judge

C. Dietz, P. Dobson, C. Delosa, C. Grandjean and T. Gerlinger. Thank you so much especially for your prayers, moral support as well as for your characteristically fraternal and sororal solicitude.

Finally, and most importantly, I express my unalloyed gratitude to my family, starting with my most beloved parents: Chief and Mrs. B.N. Anemelu to whom I owe my human generation, educational, moral and religious upbringing. Dad and Mom, I would not have been here today without you. I am likewise very grateful to all my brothers, sisters and close relations. Thank you so much for your prayers, affection, understanding, consideration, and support through this *unique* experience. I will remain eternally grateful to the Almighty God for blessing me with every single one of you. Please know how much I love you all!

DEDICATION

I dedicate this dissertation to my father, who instilled in us the desire to get good education. Above all, he was an educationist and a teacher of the first-class order himself. Likewise, I dedicate this effort to my mother, who remains, for me, a perfect model of good and benign motherhood. Dad and Mom, you both instilled discipline in us, a desire for knowledge and an understanding of the importance of learning. By extension, I dedicate project to the entire members of Anemelu family.

Finally, and in general, I would also like to dedicate work to all people of goodwill, to all those who seek to make the world a better place for every single human being on earth. Particularly, to all those who strive to promote international higher education as well as good diplomatic relations and peaceful co-existence among all nations, but more specifically to all those who endeavor to improve the quality of the life of immigrants, sojourners, refugees, aliens, international and foreign- born students' adjustment experiences across the globe.

TABLE OF CONTENTS

CHAPTER I. Introduction ... 1
    The Conceptual Framework ... 5
    Psychological Dimension ... 7
    Cultural Dimension ... 8
    Statement of the Problem ... 10
    Purpose of Study ... 13
    Research Question ... 13
    Subsidiary Questions ... 13
    Significance of Study and Relevant Implications ... 14
    Definitions and Description of Terms ... 18
    Potential Limitations of Study ... 21
    Organization of Study ... 22

CHAPTER II. Review of the Literature ... 23
    Introduction ... 23
    Historical Backdrop of FBSs' Migration for International Higher Education ... 24
    Migration and Population Impact ... 27
    Previous Literature on FBSs' Adjustment Challenges ... 29
    Basic Psycho-cultural Adaptation Issues ... 32
    Academic Maladjustment and Psychological Disorientation ... 34
    Cultural Inflexibility and Identity Consciousness ... 38
    Family Attachment and Home Nostalgia ... 47
    Psychological Adjustment ... 49

Cultural Adjustment 52
Psycho-cultural Adjustment Challenges and
Student Outcomes 56
    A. Academic Engagement/ Achievement 56
    B. Social Interaction and General Well-Being Issues 58
Summary and Evaluation 60

CHAPTER III. Research Methodology 63
Introduction 63
Method and Design 64
Population and Study Sites 65
Sample 66
Survey sampling procedure and description 66
Gender and Age 67
Year in College and Program of Studies 67
Marital and Family Status 67
Focus Group Participant Demographics 68
Gender and Age 69
Academic Programs 69
Marital and Family Presence Status 70
Instrumentation 70
Psycho-cultural Adjustment Survey 70
Focus Group Discussion Guide Questions 71
Survey and Interview Question-Guide Development 72
Contributions of the Major Pilot Survey 73
Factor Correlations 75
Reliability and Validity of Scales 75

Descriptive Factor Labels 79
Data Collection: Main Study 80
First Phase 81
Response Rates 82
Non Participants 83
Second Phase 84
Human Subjects' Protection 86
Description of Data Analysis 87
Quantitative Analysis 87
Descriptive Statistics 87
Inferential Statistics 87
Survey Questionnaire Data Analysis 88
Qualitative Analysis 89
Inductive Analysis 89
Focus Group Data Analysis 90
Data Review 91
Data Coding 92
Organizing Data 95
Categorizing Data (Responses) 95
Coding Focus Group Responses 96
Interpreting Data 96
Chapter Summary 97

CHAPTER IV. Analysis and Presentation of Findings 98
    Introduction 98
    Research Questions 98
    Organization of Chapter Contents 99

Demographic Profile of FBSs in the Survey Sample 100
Analysis of Research Questions 101
Research Question 1 101
Subscale A: Identity Consciousness and Home Nostalgia 102
Subscale B: Psychological Disorientation and Cultural Inflexibility 108
Subscale C: Family Attachment and Academic Maladjustment 113
Research Question 2 118
Analysis of Variance (ANOVA) 119
Research Question 3 131
Focus Group Session 137
Overview of Focus Group 137
Focus Group Data Analyses 138
Identity Consciousness and Home Nostalgia 138
   (A) Identity Consciousness 138
   (B) Home Nostalgia 143
Psychological Disorientation and Cultural Inflexibility 145
   (A) Psychological Disorientation 145
   (B) Cultural Inflexibility 158
Family Attachment and Academic Maladjustment 163
   (A) Family Attachment 163
   (B) Academic Maladjustment 169
Interaction among Constructs and FBSs' Adjustment Progress 179
Summary 183

CHAPTER V. Discussion, Conclusions and Recommendations 185
    Introduction 185
    Purpose of the Research 186
    Data Collection 187
    Summary of the Findings 188
    Survey Data Analyses 188
    Focus Group Data Analyses 191
    Discussion of the Findings 192
    Identity Consciousness and Home Nostalgia 192
    Psychological Disorientation and Cultural Inflexibility 195
    Family Attachment and Academic Maladjustment 201
    Conclusions from the Research Questions 205
    Research Question 1 205
    Research Question 2 207
    Research Question 3 210
    General Conclusions 212
    Implication of Findings 213
    Recommendations for Community Colleges 214
    Recommendations for Educators 215
    Recommendations for Policy Makers 215
    Recommendations for Administrators 216
    Recommendations for Counselors 217
    Future Research Directions 218
    Actual Limitations of the Present Study 220
    Concluding Remarks 222
    References 223
    Appendices 247

A. Survey Instrument		247
B. Focus Group Discussion Protocol		255

LIST OF TABLES

1. FBS Respondents sample frequency by Continents of Origin ... 68
2. Focus Group Participants Demographics ... 69
3. Reliability Coefficient Display of Primary Factor Analysis ... 75
4. Reliability Coefficient Display for PSCAQ Subscales ... 76
5. Research and Subsidiary Questions Analyses Approach ... 88
6. Coding Guide Phase One ... 93
7. Coding Guide Phase Two ... 94
8. Abridged Demographic Profile of Survey Respondents ... 100
9. Scale A: Identity Consciousness and Home Nostalgia ... 103
10. Scale B: Psychological Disorientation and Cultural Inflexibility ... 109
11. Scale C: Family Attachment and Academic Maladjustment ... 114
12. Effects of Gender on FBSs' Psycho-cultural Adjustment (ANOVA) ... 120
13. Effects of FBSs' Age on their Psycho-cultural Adjustment (ANOVA) ... 122
14. Effects of Marital Status on FBSs' Psycho-cultural Adjustment (ANOVA) ... 125
15. Effects of Continents of Origin on FBSs' Psycho-cultural Adjustment (ANOVA) ... 126

16. Effects of Year in College on FBSs' Psycho-cultural Adjustment (ANOVA) ... 128
17. Effects of Family Presence on FBSs' Psycho-cultural Adjustment (ANOVA) ... 130
18. Frequency Distribution for Items 37- 44 (Outcome Variable) ... 132
19. Select Items Addressing Research Question 3 ... 136

LIST OF FIGURES

1. Proposed Psycho-Cultural Research Model Conceptual Framework … 7
2. Bar Chart Display: Plans to continue study at the CC … 134
3. Bar Chart Display: Plans to return after studies at the CC … 134
4. Bar Chart Display: Feelings to drop out of the CC … 134
5. Bar Chart Display: Plans to enroll in a 4 year college university on Completion … 134
6. Bar Chart Display: Satisfaction with life at the CC … 135
7. Bar Chart Display: Re-selecting the CC for studies … 135
8. Bar Chart Display: Re-selecting the US for further studies … 135
9. Bar Chart Display: Recommending the US for studies to others in their countries … 135

CHAPTER I
Introduction

Academic opportunities are among the reasons individuals consider studying in the United States (US) irrespective of their academic interests. Whether they desire a large, small, or medium-sized institution, unlimited options are available in the US. For students from foreign countries the US has become a country of major attraction to such an extent that both students and scholars perceive higher education in the US as the best system in the world (Altbach, 2004; Johnson, 1993; Keller, 1983; Trow, 1989). For the purpose of clarity, the term *foreign-born students* (FBSs) has been adopted in this study to incorporate as well as substitute for *international students* (ISs), which in the US context, have been defined as not only all those from other countries who come to the US for the primary purpose of obtaining a degree but also as foreign students who temporarily stay in the US to accomplish their educational goals (Bahvala, 2002; Robertson, Line, Jones, & Thomas, 2000; Sakurako, 2000).

Foreign-born students constitute a growingly relevant and salient source of diversity on college and university campuses. From an economic perspective enrolling substantial numbers of FBSs generate tremendous revenue for the US. According to the US Department of Commerce FBSs contribute nearly $20 billion to the US economy through their expenditures on tuition and living expenses (Open Doors, 2010). Enrollment of FBSs also benefits American students in the marketplace to the extent that their cultural sensitivities and skills in working with people from different backgrounds are augmented (Calleja, 2000; Carnevale,

1999). The Institute of International Education reported during the 2009-2010 academic year the number of FBSs who studied at colleges and universities in the US increased by 3% over the prior year to 690,923 signifying a record high number of FBSs in the US. According to Open Doors report (2011), 732, 277 FBSs studied in the US in the 2010-2011 academic year, the highest number in the US history. This was 5.7% higher than the previous year. Despite the global economic downturn, this all-time-high increase speaks to the quality and diversity ascribable to the US system of higher education around the world coupled with unparalleled opportunities it offers for creativity, flexibility, and cultural exchange (IIE, 2011).

The US has a highly decentralized system that gives students a wide range of educational options from large universities to two-year colleges (Spellings, 2005). Community colleges (CCs) in particular, have been conceived as the gateway to higher education in the US for a growing number of students. They provide virtually open access to anyone who has completed secondary education or has the equivalent of a high school diploma. These two-year colleges are available to individuals of varied age ranges. With an open door policy (Clark, 1960), CCs provide students with an opportunity to earn credits for the first two years of a four-year bachelor's degree. They are often characterized by lower tuition costs thereby enhancing affordability while providing learning in a college environment.

Interestingly, community colleges also constitute the first stop for roughly half of today's college students. Cox (2009) found that CCs are often treated as adjunct to US higher education or even placed at the bottom tier of a strictly differentiated system of higher education.

Nevertheless, they comprise the largest group of different types of accredited post-secondary institutions as well as play a central role in granting access to the same system of US higher education. CCs are the largest and fastest-growing sector of higher education in the US. There are close to 1,200 regionally accredited CCs located throughout the US, serving about 11 million students and accounting for approximately 44 percent of all US undergraduates (AACC, 2012). Foreign-born (international) student enrollments at CCs have also been on the rise in recent years. During the 2006-2007, academic year 84,061 foreign-born students were enrolled in CCs in the US. In 2007-2008, CCs in the US enrolled 86,683 FBSs. The 2008-2009 academic year saw CCs in the US enroll 95,785. Records indicate that CCs experienced a 10.5 percent growth in foreign-born (international) student enrollment in the 2008-2009 academic year, the highest of any type of higher education institution. More than 94,000 FBSs were enrolled in CCs in 2009-2010; only a negligible percentage in decline (Open Doors, 2011).

Given the unprecedented national expansion in the number of community colleges and in their foreign-born student enrollment, CCs across the country face the complex task of preparing a diverse array of students, who represent an assorted set of learning needs, for success within the classroom and the community. In addition, FBSs themselves face their own career development challenges. There does not seem to be any one method for approaching these challenges, nor any common solution to confronting the hindrances to learning and career development faced by FBSs as they move along their educational and career paths (Harper & Quaye, 2009).

Moreover, for foreign-born students adjusting to a new

environment and lifestyle can be quite psychologically demanding and even culturally difficult. This is because new circumstances naturally impose a variety of competing roles and demands on their arrival into a new country. FBSs face other potential challenges such as adjusting to other cultures and a complicated series of crises connected to entering colleges and universities, as well as the challenge of keeping in touch with their own identity (Barletta & Kobayashi, 2007). Therefore, the challenge for an FBS is to learn quickly while at the same time trying to adapt to a new academic environment (Stabb, Harris, & Talley, 1995).

The main thesis of this study is that peoples' ability to adjust to a new culture and social environment is influenced by their previously acquired, internalized as well as shared values, beliefs, attitudes, myths, legends, norms, convictions, assumptions, ideologies, principles, and self-concept. These elements are encapsulated in their inner struggles with new cultures and environment as a result of the special meanings, importance and perspectives they accord to certain elements and issues in their native culture (Adler, 2002; Belozersky, 1990; Fritz, Chin & DeMarinis, 2008; Mishal & Morag, 2002; Ross, 2001). This reality ultimately finds expression in their patterns of thinking, feelings, and behaviors (self-presentation) as they adjust to a new culture and social environment. This constellation of values, attitudes, beliefs, attributes, principles, ideologies, assumptions, worldview, experiences and outlook is sometimes referred to indirectly as identity (Adler, 2002; Benhabib, 1999; Chen, 1999; Ross, 2001).

The above psycho-cultural conceptual rationale provides a foundation and framework for the current investigation of foreign-born students' adjustment challenges at community colleges. This rationale both informs the challenges and perhaps constitutes the ancillary driver of all other challenges that FBSs face thereby making it a special target for an in-depth study. Therefore, examining the psycho-cultural adjustment challenges facing FBSs at CCs is deeply informed by the subsequent review of relevant psycho-cultural theories, and their basic dimensions.

The Conceptual Framework

Figure 1 portrays the conceptual framework and guiding structure for this investigation. This unique construction advances a model for examining psycho-cultural adjustment challenges of foreign-born students at community colleges in the Northeastern US. This psycho-cultural research model also includes other more specific concepts that serve as indicators and predictors of potential psycho-cultural maladjustment propensities among FBSs at CCs. It depicts the integration of rationales that produced the psycho-cultural phenomenon under study. This integration is primarily guided as well as informed by a confluence of beliefs, attitudes, values, myths, norms, legends, customs, convictions, philosophical assumptions, and ideologies latently accumulated and internalized over time by FBSs. It serves to hold the parts of this study together, represents ideas that give structure to the process of this research study, and provides it with vision, coherence and direction. This conceptual framework was developed from deep cross-cultural dimensional theories that present underlying structures of culture with proven psycho-cultural undertones (Adler, 2002; Belozersky, 1990; Conover, 2009; Hogg & Williams, 2000; Neuliep, 2008; Oyserman, Coon & Kemmelmier, 2002; Quatroche, 2000; Ross, 2001; Samovar, Porter, &

Stephani, 2000; Singelis, 2000; Toomey, 1999; Triandis, 2002; Trompenaars & Hampden-Turner, 1998).

The first tier of this basically triangulated exhibit displays two major components of the psycho-cultural concept: psychological dimension and the cultural dimension. They provided origin to this conceptual rationale. The second tier presents us with the core descriptive categories of the psycho-cultural concept. They embody those major unquantifiable factors that negatively influence foreign-born students' adjustment. They include ethnocentrism, xenocentrism, individualism, collectivism, prejudice, and stereotypes. The third tier outlines the characteristics, indicators, and potential predictors of psycho-cultural maladjustment among FBSs in a new culture and environment. They refer to psychological disorientation, cultural inflexibility, identity consciousness, family attachment, home nostalgia and academic maladjustment.

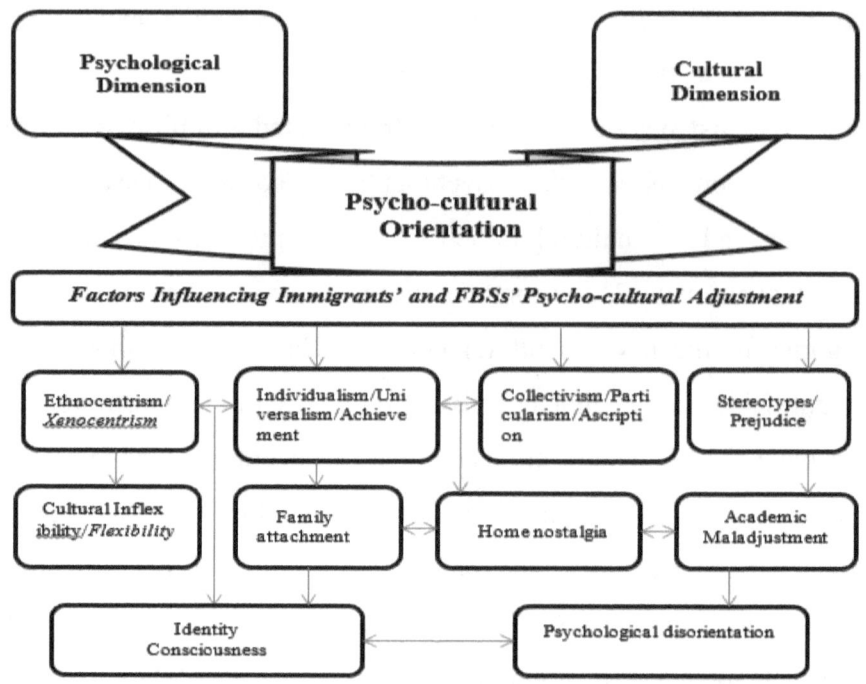

Figure 1. Proposed Psycho-cultural Research Model Conceptual Framework

Psychological Dimension

Dozens of studies have viewed the development of identity as related to cognitive or psychological development and the search for identity as ongoing throughout adolescence into adulthood. The first step in identity development is establishing the integrity of the personality; that is, aligning emotions, thinking and behavior to be consistent regardless of place, time, circumstances and social relationships (Breger, 2009; Kroger, 2000; Moshman, 2005; Steinberg & Morris, 2001). As foreign-born students navigate the predominantly US college and university educational environment they encounter as well as grapple with numerous psychological barriers in their struggle to become well-adjusted (Bahvala, 2002; Burrel & Kim, 2002; Chen, 1999; Ciguralova, 2005; Mori, 2000;

Sakurako, 2000; Tatar & Horenczyck, 2003; Tseng & Newton, 2002; Yi, Lin & Kishimoto, 2003). It should, therefore, not be taken for granted that self-identity, as well as collective identity on FBSs' adjustment to a new environment and culture is influenced by some deep-rooted cultural factors.

Cultural Dimension

Both cross-cultural and multi-cultural research has also shown that individual nations, from which foreign-born students come, have their uniquely dominant and predominant cultural identities. Research has, for instance, revealed important distinctions between the collectivist cultures typically found in Africa, Asia, and Latin America and the individualistic cultures more commonly found in North America and Europe (Heine et al., 2001; Hogg & Williams, 2000; Singelis, 2000). These findings illustrate two contrasting cultural orientations in which most people, including FBSs in the US colleges and universities, discover their own identities. One values individualism and the virtues of independence, autonomy, and self-reliance, the other orientation values collectivism and the virtues of interdependence, cooperation, and social harmony. In collectivist cultures, the person is first, a loyal member of a family, team, company, church, and state. Under the banner of individualism, by contrast, one's personal goals take priority over group allegiances. Individualism and collectivism are so deeply ingrained in a culture that they mold peoples' very self-conceptions and identities (Conover, 2009; Toomey, 1999). Most North Americans and Europeans have an independent view of the self. In this perspective, the self is an entity that is distinct, autonomous, self-contained, and endowed with unique dispositions. Yet, in much of Asia, Africa, and Latin America, people hold an interdependent view of the self (Brehm, Kassim, & Fein, 2002; Oyserman, Coon & Kemmelmier, 2002; Triandis, 2002).

A growing body of research suggests that foreign-born students often experience cultural and other social challenges in connection with their struggle to adjust to a new environment in colleges and universities here in the US (Chen, 1999; Gloria & Ho, 2003; Rajapaksa & Dundes, 2003; Nilsson & Anderson, 2004; Schmitt, Spears & Branscombe, 2003; Stromquist & Monkman, 2000; Tomich, McWhirter, & Darcy, 2003; Toyokawa & Toyokawa, 2002; Tseng & Newton, 2002; Ward, Bochner & Furnham, 2001).

Psychological and cultural orientation perspectives have provided an integrated theoretical leverage for understanding the psycho-cultural adjustment challenges that foreign-born students face at community colleges. The established conceptual rationale reveals complex interconnections between the psychological and cultural factors that are encapsulated in the psycho-cultural research framework discussed above. Overall structural factors in the form of an integrated psychological and cultural orientation which produced the psycho-cultural construct also provide a context that constrains the degree to which individual factors (personality influences, etc.) can either be discounted or taken into account (Adler, 2002; Belozersky, 1990; Hazen & Alberts, 2006; Kim & Omizzo, 2001; Kim & Gudykunst, 1992).

Structural factors such as psychological development, social, educational, and cultural differences between the US and a given foreign-born student's home country, set up a framework that is common to most students from that country. Onto this psycho-cultural framework (psychological plus cultural orientation) is layered a host of factors specific to the individual, and groups (Belozersky, 1990; Blair-Brocker & Ernst, 2000; Kim & Gudykunst, 1992; Kosic, 2002; LIobera, 2003; Neuliep, 2008; Plotnik, 2002; Portes & Madelon, 2001; Quatroche, 1999; Ross, 2001; Samovar et al., 2000; Wade & Travis, 2000; Ward & Kennedy, 2001; Ward & Ran-Deuba, 1999; Zakaria, 2000). These factors include characteristics of the individual's personal, cultural, and group identity, as well as previously acquired and assimilated values. This single psycho-cultural conceptual perspective will be employed in this study of foreign-born students' adjustment challenges at community colleges.

Statement of the Problem

With rare exceptions the legal acquisition of student visas for further studies in a foreign land qualifies a foreign-born student as an "international student" (IS) in a strictly regulated sense. A glimpse of academic experience in the foreign country and program of choice could also convince the student of the pleasant nature and quality of institution in the chosen country of sojourn. However, this would certainly depend on an individual student's disposition, aspirations, and expectations as well as experiences with the campus climate. The majority of foreign-born students find in the US a special place to advance their studies and consequently consider it a land of opportunities (Florida, 2005; Grusky, 2000).

On a different note, foreign-born students face a wide range of adjustment challenges as they migrate and increase in number. In a similar vein, growth in immigrant student populations of urban community colleges in recent years creates new challenges for college counselors because counseling intervention is essential for FBSs to cope with the stresses of immigration and the effects of these stresses on their college performance (Brilliant, 2000). These challenges could simply be categorized as psychological, cultural, academic, and social. Each aspect of these challenges can find expression in the various needs and commitments of FBSs such as, academic adjustment, linguistic, social interaction, financial, immigration, housing and other environmental adaptation issues. Previous studies on foreign-born students' adjustment in another country, mostly conducted in the four-year colleges and university setting, reflect five general tendencies in the literature: cultural, psychological, social, academic, and environmental models. Most of the literature indicated that studies in a foreign land create enormous level of stress, anxiety, depression, and feelings of loneliness (Bahvala, 2002; Burrel & Kim, 2002; Chen, 1999; Ciguralova, 2005; Mori, 2000; Sakurako, 2000; Tatar & Horenczyck, 2003; Tseng & Newton, 2002; Yi, Lin & Kishimoto, 2003). Most research tend to focus on cultural adjustment issues as well as on differences in cultural norms and practices without delving deeper into its connection with the psychological adjustment (Chen, 1999; Harthshone & Baucom, 2007; Gloria & Ho, 2003; Nilsson & Anderson, 2004; Rajapaksa & Dundes, 2003; Schmitt, Spears & Branscombe, 2003; Stromquist & Monk man, 2000; Tomich, McWhirter & Darcy, 2003; Toyokawa & Toyokawa, 2002; Tseng & Newton, 2002; Ward, Bochner & Furnham, 2001).

Indeed, not much has been done to explore the psycho-cultural adjustment challenges that foreign-born students may be facing at higher institutions of learning, especially, CCs. This present study which emphasizes the importance of studying FBSs' adaptation at CCs, from a psycho-cultural perspective, will help to fill this gap. However, the post-migration psycho-cultural challenges that IS face in higher institutions of learning, especially community colleges, have not been easy to establish. Unlike other challenges, psycho-cultural adjustment transcends the merely observable because they are not only based on the deeper structure of cultural identity, values, beliefs, attitudes, and norms internalized over time, but also on the special (unconventional) meaning and interpretation accorded to certain cultural elements as well as situations by an individual or groups (Adler, 2002; Ross, 2001).

The integration of both psychological and cultural elements into an explanation for foreign-born students' adjustment challenges is far more useful than reliance on either alone why a psycho-cultural perspective seeks to explain challenges and conflicts linked to culturally learned dispositions and the interpretations of the world (Mishal & Morag, 2002; Ross, 2001). Therefore, explaining the psycho-cultural in this study as opposed to the merely psychological or cultural emphasizes assumptions, perceptions, and images about the world that are widely shared by participants from the same social and cultural system (Volkan, 1999). This research was undertaken from a standpoint of generating information that might be relevant towards addressing the special needs of this heterogeneous group of students.

Purpose of Study

The purpose of this study is to examine post-migration psycho-cultural adjustment challenges faced by foreign-born students at community colleges. This explanatory mixed method study therefore hopes to change the ways in which various needs of FBSs at CCs are being assessed as well as addressed. In this project I will present a psycho-cultural model encapsulating aspects of the psychological and cultural orientations that potentially constitute barriers to FBSs' adjustment at CCs.

The focus of this research is not just about what foreign-born students do or how they interact in a given environment but more about why they think, feel, present, or self-identify (assess) themselves, as well as interpret events as they strive to adjust to a new college environment. It is assumed that these dispositions are deep-seated, socially constructed internal representations of the self, others, and one's social world (Schramm-Nielsen, 2002). This study identifies major factors that explain the post-migration psycho-cultural adjustment challenges among FBSs in the context under study. It is a study that may contribute to previous thoughts about FBSs' adjustment challenges.

The Research Question

To what extent and in what ways do FBSs enrolled in CCs in the US face post-migration psycho-cultural adjustment challenges?

Subsidiary Questions

1. To what extent in what ways do post-migration psycho-cultural adjustment challenges differ among groups of FBSs (such as gender, age,

year in college, continent of origin, marital status and family presence) enrolled in CCs in the US?

2. To what extent and in what ways are post-migration psycho-cultural adjustment challenges related to the outcomes (Social Interaction and Academic/Career Engagement) of FBSs' adjustment at CCs in the US?

Significance of Study and Relevant Implications

Without doubt, the push and pull of globalization drives students to pursue higher education outside their own countries, especially here in the US and people, certainly, leap at this opportunity. Institutions in the US enroll the highest number of foreign-born (international) students accounting for about 28% in the world (Bain & Cummings, 2005; Mazzarol & Soutar, 2002; OECD, 2002). FBSs' arrival and enrollment at community colleges and other higher institutions of learning in the US naturally and logically presuppose migration as well as anticipate student life on campus along with challenges of whatsoever description on a foreign soil. Since the issue of FBSs' adjustment not only evokes but also presupposes migration and mobility, a brief but profound review of available literature on the migration and mobility of FBSs might significantly clear grounds for a better investigation of FBSs' potential post-migration psycho-cultural adjustment challenges at CCs. This is because the issue of international higher education which entails, first and foremost, migration (mobility) and then student adjustment has been necessarily and reasonably implicated in this study.

Admittedly, there are aspects of higher education that remain under-studied and inadequately understood (Bystritsky, 2006; Giangreco,

2010). The same is applicable to certain students' life and challenges on campus that either have been previously unknown or insufficiently studied among which belong post-migration psycho-cultural variables (factors) that may have been impacting foreign-born students' adjustment on campus. Even though without direct reference to FBSs at CCs or their psycho-cultural adjustment challenges, researchers have variously alluded to discussions about students' migration, mobility, diversity, life challenges and their implications, addressing them as among those aspects of higher education that remain either underexplored or inadequately studied (Brettel & Hollifield, 2000; Cox, 2009;King & Ruis-Gelices, 2003; Papastergiadis, 2000; Sakurako, 2000). Some of these writings further illuminate various aspects of the student life and challenges that unfold across higher education levels, inside CCs and, by extension, throughout higher education writ large. It is these aforementioned rings of thought and conceptions that gave further fillip to my choice of investigating FBSs' post-migration adjustment challenges at CCs from a psycho-cultural viewpoint.

Understanding post-migration psycho-cultural adjustment challenges that foreign-born students potentially face at community colleges is important for several reasons. Firstly, it might reveal details of what may have been the possible root cause(s) of FBSs' maladjustment in certain areas of traditional students' life on campus which among others are classified as psychological, cultural, academic, and social. Secondly, for the benefit of conflict resolution and problem-solving, it might open up new but unique perspectives in the ways FBSs' adjustment challenges have been handled for decades in higher institutions of learning. Furthermore, a clear appreciation of those perspectives might lead to a possible revisit of how FBSs' adjustment challenges are being addressed in various colleges and universities at present. This type of initiative might offer educators, administrators, policy makers, and directors of FBSs' affairs the leverage to strategize better in modifying services provided to these groups of students not only during their orientation programs but also throughout their stay on campus.

Therefore, the American higher education system must not only do more to deeply study the modes of thought, feelings, attitudes, assumptions, perception, values, and the cultures of people from other nations, it is also increasingly expedient for administrators, faculty and staff as well as American students at CCs to be aware of the potential presence and special post-migration psycho-cultural needs of FBSs in their midst. This expediency cannot be overemphasized. With each passing year, it grows more obvious that colleges must prepare Americans to deal more competently with people from other parts of the globe. It will also help us to determine whether or not American culture needs to become less ethnocentric, more or less patronizing, less individualistic, less pragmatic, less utilitarian and less ignorant of others, less Manichean in judging other cultures, and more at home with the rest of the world (Yankelovich, 2005).

This explanatory study aims to contribute to the already existing body of literature on foreign-born students by conceptually integrating the psychological and cultural adjustment challenges of FBSs in this project. The significance will therefore flow from studying to transcending generalizations of the available research literature on foreign- born student adjustment. I do believe that one of the reasons potential post-migration psycho-cultural adjustment challenges of FBSs have been relatively unknown or overlooked is partly because much emphasis has instead been laid on the factors that motivate their immigration and the benefits they take away (Mazzarol & Soutar, 2002). The research findings will also have relevant implications across several levels. First of all, it will help educators in higher education to develop a better understanding of how FBSs differ from their American counterparts and in determining ways to assist these students in adjusting to their host (American) culture. My goal now is to raise the level of knowledge and discussion on FBSs in tertiary institutions, add to literature on the topic, and highlight cultural diversity affecting their psychological, cultural, academic, and even social adaptation to the community and society. This project will contribute to an ever-greater recognition of FBSs as a positively special element of the higher education system not only here in the US but in other countries also. It is crucial to re-emphasize that in this research study FBSs is not only used interchangeably with the term *international students* but also comprise all those who came into US from other countries as well as cultures and are currently studying at community colleges.

In order for the US to retain its attractiveness as a host country and to better accommodate the significant number of foreign-born students studying at community colleges it is essential to identify and understand the challenges that this segment of the student population faces as well as appreciate them for who and what they are. Policy makers and college administrators in particular may need to be more aware of the challenges and struggles of these students. Such awareness might help the government and institutions to identify the adjustment needs of FBSs, reduce their frustrations, disappointments, and challenges they might be facing and posing for student affairs administrators when dealing with their transitional problems as FBSs. It will also provide professionals with guidelines for developing a psycho-cultural education, appropriate for services and programs that lay much emphasis on the psycho-cultural by highlighting the roles of culture-specific, community-based resources (Cigularova, 2005; Voison & Dillon-Remy, 2002).

Definitions and Description of Terms

Adjustment challenges: Refer to the problems faced by FBSs as they strive to adapt to a new culture and environment other than their own.

Academic maladjustment: Refers to a certain difficulty that FBSs' may have adjusting to class and academic demands in a different culture and environment.

Community college (CC): Refers to a two-year public institution of higher education in the US.

Culture: Refers to patterns of behavior, values and shared ways of living by groups of individuals.

Cultural challenges: Refer to the problems faced by FBSs as they endeavor to adapt to other people's shared values and ways of life.

Cultural identity: Refers to the values, attitudes, beliefs and ways of life with which FBSs associate themselves.

Culture inflexibility: Refers to FBSs' rigid adherence to issues related to their original ways of life, manners, philosophical assumptions, values, customs, attitudes, and beliefs.

Ethnocentrism: Refers to attitudinally defensive tendencies and perceptions toward values, norms of one's own culture and ways of living as superior to and more reasonable and appropriate than those of others.

Family attachment: Refers to irrational and unbridled family affiliations by FBSs following relocation to a different environment and culture away from their own home.

Foreign-born students (FBSs): Refers to students from other countries, other than the United States, who are enrolled in community colleges in the United States and who were not born and raised in the United States. This may include immigrants, refugees, holders of F (student) visas, H (temporary worker/trainee) visas, J (temporary educational exchange-visitor) visas, R (Religious) visas and M (vocational training) visas.

Home nostalgia: Refers to FBSs' sentimental longing for home, keen interest as well as deep memory of things and past experiences from home. It is simply intense yearning for what is missed at home.

Identity consciousness: Refers to individual value connections based on a constant definition and identification of oneself as a unique individual, in terms of roles, attitudes, culture, beliefs and aspirations (Berger, 2001). Refers to how FBSs constantly present themselves in relationship to a new culture and environment.

Immigrants (immigrant students): Refer to all those students who were born outside of the US and who are currently studying in any higher institutions of learning in the US or simply resident or working in the US and who do not have the intention of going back to their home countries. This may include holders of permanent resident visas, and those who possess citizenship status by naturalization. For the purpose of this study, immigrant students may also be referred to as FBSs or used interchangeably.

International students (ISs): These incorporate all students from other countries, aside from the US, who are currently studying at CCs in the US. However, in some cases, foreign-born students or immigrant students will be used interchangeably for international students (ISs) in this project because even though ISs are officially temporary migrants, many eventually become immigrants to the US (Arum & Van de Water, 1992; Bahvala, 2002; Borjas, 2002; Harari, 1992; Hazen & Alberts, 2006; Robertson, Line, Jones, & Thomas, 2000; Sakurako, 2000).

Migration: Refers to the movement or mobility of FBSs from their country of birth (place of origin) to another.

Personal well-being: Refers to individual's good physical, emotional and psychological health as well as comfort and happiness in a given environment.

Prejudice: Refers to the judgment and decisions FBSs make about things, events or situations based on their self-conception, belief system, previous experiences, perceptions, and assumptions.

Psychological disorientation: Refers to the unhealthy mental impact of being immersed in a new environment and of adjustment to a place that is different from one's own country of origin due to previously accumulated deep cultural values.

Psycho-cultural: Refers to a confluence of acquired and shared values, attitudes, norms, beliefs, customs, assumptions, ideologies, principles, convictions as well as myths and legends that influence one's thoughts, feelings and actions. These are summarized in the larger issue of identity or the presentation of oneself or a group in a new environment and culture. It often finds expression in the special meanings individuals and groups assign to persons, issues, events, and things.

Socio-cultural: Refers to the interaction of social and cultural elements that reveal the social and cultural aspects of an individual or group behavior in a society.

Stereotypes: Refers to a fixed set of ideas (perceptions) FBSs may have about issues, events, things, and persons that are, in most cases, not objective.

Xenocentrism: Refers to some inferiority complex arising from a deep-rooted belief that other people's culture and values are superior to one's own culture and values.

Potential Limitations of Study

This study will be conducted at only three community colleges in the Northeastern US. The study will focus on the post-migration psycho-cultural adjustment challenges that foreign-born students may have been facing at CCs. It will anticipate certain variables that might impact FBSs' total response to a survey questionnaire and focus group discussion schedule. This study examines only the psycho-cultural challenges that FBSs may be facing at CCs here in the US. It does not extend itself to the pre-arrival challenges of FBSs.

It is important to note that data and information will be elicited based on individual feelings, thoughts, assumptions, perceptions, opinions and experiences of FBSs at the three participating CCs in the Northeastern US, which may not be all-representative of objective reality. Any data analysis that examines variables and their effects, despite reliability of data collection, may not always provide definitive assurance of all-data accuracy in this original study. This implies that since this research involves a mixed-method approach which includes a cross-sectional survey application, responses to survey items cannot always be taken as accurate descriptions of what the respondents actually do, think or really feel about a phenomenon.

Organization of Study

I conducted a mixed method research on the post-migration psycho-cultural adjustment challenges that foreign-born students face at community colleges. In the pursuit of this objective I approached it in five chapters. Chapter I begins with the introduction, followed by a triangulated psycho-cultural conceptual rationale with both the psychological and cultural orientations forming the basic building block of this psycho-cultural framework, statement of purpose, the significance of study, research questions, subsidiary questions and definition of terms and the limitations of the study. Chapter II delves into an overview and historical background of international education, the impact of migration and the mobility of foreign-born students, the review of literature, theories, and concepts, related to FBSs' adjustment at universities and colleges including community colleges. In Chapter III, I reviewed the methodology employed in this study. In Chapter IV, the findings and the analysis of the investigation are presented. Chapter V completes the project by providing conclusions, implications for practice, and recommendations for future research.

CHAPTER II
Review of the Literature

Introduction

An in-depth review of any adjustment challenges facing foreign-born students at community colleges would require some concise comprehension of how international migration for higher education (international studies) in general came about. This type of understanding and historical backdrop will help provide context for consideration of the nature of challenges facing FBSs, as well as give this research and literature review a sharpened focus. The expected outcome of this research, which will be highlighted in this literature review is, primarily, to prove if indeed there are potential post-migration psycho-cultural adjustment challenges among FBSs at CCs in the Northeastern US. Secondly, it is to show to what extent and in what ways identified potential post-migration psycho-cultural variables (indicators/identifiers) are correlated to various aspects of FBSs' adjustment challenges at the participating community colleges. This includes among others the academic, social life, college enrollment, engagement, and retention of FBSs.

This literature review is therefore divided into four major sections: The first section comprises a brief history and review of the foreign-born students' migration for higher education as well as the population impact of those migrations. The second section presents a review of previous literature, theories, and studies on the basic psycho-cultural adaptation issues with the subsections focusing on FBSs' psychological and cultural adjustments. Section three takes an in depth look into the psycho-cultural adjustment and students' adaptability outcomes broken down into academic engagement, social interaction, and general well-being issues of FBSs with relevant psycho-cultural underpinnings. Finally, section four offers a summary and evaluation of the whole study and the entire range of literature. All these sections are reviewed from a broader context of psycho-cultural adjustment challenges of FBSs.

Historical Backdrop of FBSs' Migration for International Higher Education

The mere mention of foreign-born students' adjustment challenges evokes the issue of mobility (migration from their own country of origin to another) which is clearly an important global phenomenon. Apart from mobility programs, globalization, and migration are also parts of the reasons why the scope of higher education has completely changed over the past decades thus enabling increased contact of diverse cultures (Emuni Higher Education & Research Proceedings, 2009). Borrowing from a broad range of theoretical debates and current trends in sociology, anthropology, geography, political economy, and cultural analysis, mobility has been severally described as not only a product of globalization but also as a key feature of contemporary life leading to cardinal changes in our profound understanding of culture, identity and community (Altbach & Teichler, 2001; Papastergiadis, 2000). However, literature is scant on the mobility of FBSs because geographers and others interested in population mobility have been remarkably slow to study the migration behavior of this increasingly numerous and strategically significant fraction of the student population (Brettel & Hollifield, 2000; King & Ruis-Gelices, 2003; Papastergiadis, 2000).

Studies on foreign-born students' migration remain limited in number with great concentration on the initial migration-flows resulting from the decision to study abroad and on the return or non-return of graduates to their country of origin at the end of their foreign study programs (King & Ruis-Gelices, 2003). Some of the available literature concentrates on FBSs' migration during their study programs and specifically on their year abroad.

Schuster and Finkelstein (2006) aptly note that since a group of unhappy scholars in Paris defected to found a collegium across the channel in Oxford, centuries have witnessed incessant transnational (international) movements of scholars and students. This sounds like a historically informed report on the nature of exchanges in conjunction with segments of societies. More specifically the particular illustrations are: the mobility of scholars and students within Europe, the idea of wandering scholars, and revolutions around the world. Each of them certainly exemplifies the implication of international education and studies upon societies. While referring to the United States as an exporter of scholars and students during the last quarter of the nineteenth century eager to pursue advanced studies in Europe, especially at the more evolved German universities, Schuster and Finkelstein (2006) stressed that the US also became a huge net importer of scholars in the twentieth century. This observation certainly presents and re-presents higher education as having transcended national borders through the movement of more students and scholars into and outside of the United States. For the purpose of this study, concentration will be strictly placed on the migration and mobility of students in an international or transnational context. It is striking at this point to note that activities and programs that encourage the flow of ideas and people across cultural and international boundaries have been summarized as international studies/education (Arum & Van de Water, 1992; Harari, 1992). In line with this summary and for later literature review on this project, the international or transnational movement of students has also been given as the definition of International Student Exchange Program (Harari, 1992, p. 69). This definition might be somewhat helpful since foreign-born students in this research also includes those who engage or participate in international student exchange programs as much as it incorporates scholars in this introductory literature review on migration and mobility to highlight further and advanced studies.

Altbach and Teichler (2001), citing Geiger (1986), observed that Americans as foreign-born students traveled to Germany in the late nineteenth century to obtain doctoral degrees returning to the United States imbued with the importance of research as an integral part of the university. In this connection Americans returned from their academic 'Mecca' in Germany, much as students from the Third World now return from Western universities, fired with enthusiasm for the academic traditions and ideas they experienced during their formative student days. Even though this work presented a refreshingly frank and balanced picture of the how and the purpose of FBSs' migration for higher education, there is little interest shown in the challenges that FBSs faced let alone their potential post-migration psycho-cultural adjustment challenges. This volume is simply an historical report that provides concise information on the how and why some of the American students participated in study abroad that entailed crossing national borders.

In recent years foreign-born students' migration is believed to have grown significantly in a context characterized by the internationalization of tertiary education and the development of new information and communication technologies (Dia, 2005). It should not be overlooked that the idea of migration and mobility for FBSs logically provokes issues of population and demographics. Institutions in the United States consider the population of FBSs as increasingly important as the nation has become ever more dependent on these students in several ways (Altbach & Teichler, 2001). This dependence is further elucidated in the *World Educational Services Review* (2007) that upholds that FBSs hold several short and long term gains for institutions and developed countries like the US in their strategic economic development from the perspectives of financial revenue and cultural diversity promotion. The same dependence has necessitated current implementation of further initiatives to facilitate the arrival and integration of overseas students, including substantial amendments to immigration requirements and procedures (Verbik & Lasanowski, 2007; *World Educational Services Review*, 2007).

Migration and Population Impact

The impact of peoples' migration (mobility) along with ideas and capital across the globe has been traced in some literature with a striking discovery of dramatic changes in the identity and experience of migrants through history. There has been a claim of more people being on the move with their destination uncertain and journeys more complex than ever before (Dia, 2005; King & Ruis-Gelices, 2003; Papastergiadis, 2000). Despite various adjustment challenges following their global movements,

FBSs seem to have been relatively successful in navigating the passageways to higher education attainment (Chen, 2008; Davis, 1998; WES, 2007). Over the past 13-18 years international student mobility has become a pivotal portion of the global higher education landscape. The total number of mobile tertiary education students was estimated to have reached more than 2.7 million in 2005, a nearly 61% increase since 1999 (Verbik & Lasanowski, 2007). Such a dramatic change in such a short time is partly explicable by significant changes in the infrastructure and capacity of higher education systems across the globe. Traditionally, more than 90 percent of FBSs have enrolled in institutions in countries belonging to the Organization for Economic Co-operation and Development (OECD) with the main destinations (United States, United Kingdom, Germany, France, and Australia) recruiting over 70% of them (Verbik & Lasanowski, 2007; World Education Services, 2007).

Davis (1998) gives a general description of the foreign-born students' population in the latter part of the twentieth century by noting that more than half of the FBSs' population was from Asia and this proportion continues to increase. In addition, about one third of the international student population was then comprised of women. Most were in four-year institutions while about two thirds were in the public schools. This is a survey report done in the late part of the twentieth century by the International Education of American academic institutions concerning FBSs. Clearly FBSs continue to have an impact on colleges and universities across the United States, an impact that is growing in magnitude. Because of this trend it has become ever more important to understand this subpopulation of students especially in our community colleges, to be able to assess and address their needs as well as recognize their importance. Psychological, cultural, and environmental adjustments are among the first problems that are typically faced by FBSs following migration.

Chen (2008) observes that in our modern world characterized by globalization the responsibility of CCs for producing high quality competence can neither be overlooked nor overemphasized. This article did not lay much stress on foreign-born students at community colleges, neither did it delve into the issue of adjustment challenges facing FBSs at CCs. Rather it reported research on international education and provides insight on the significance of community college educators. His study involved quantitative and qualitative approaches to topics of international education. He made a special report, while citing open doors that, in the academic year 2005-2006, 83,160 FBSs were enrolled in CCs while 4,823 students from American CCs went abroad to study during the academic year 2004-2005. Having reviewed completed dissertations on international education at CCs from the year 2002 to 2007, he stressed only the need to increase the study of international education in CCs (Chen, 2008).

Previous Literature on FBSs' Adjustment Challenges

Research as well as related theories and concepts on international student adjustment challenges has demonstrated that certain cultural, social and psychological factors influence foreign-born students' adjustment to a foreign culture and environment. Some of these problems are related to cultural conflicts, psychological distress, loneliness, homesickness, social maladaptation, difficulty accommodating new roles, academic and language difficulties (Bahvala, 2002; Burrel & Kim, 2002;

Chen, 1999; Ciguralova, 2005; Mori, 2000; Rajapaksa & Dundes, 2002; Sakurako, 2000; Tatar & Horenczyck, 2003; Tseng & Newton, 2002; Yi, Lin & Kishimoto, 2003). While previous literature also attempted to explore the socio-cultural dimensions (Li & Gasser, 2005; Wang & Frank, 2002; Ward & Kennedy, 2001) as well as the psycho-social (Ciguralova, 2005; Kaczmarek, Matlock, Merta, Ames, & Ross 1994; Lin & Yi, 1997; Pedersen, 1995; Wang & Mallinckrodt, 2006) dimensions of FBSs' adjustment challenges, little or no attention has been paid to the psycho-cultural constructs of their adjustment challenges in the literature. Previous other studies have also been conducted precisely on the psychological adjustment challenges and needs of FBSs at four-year colleges and universities coupled with few other studies outside of the community college setting on the psycho-cultural adjustment challenges. (Bahvala, 2002; Chen, 1999; 2004; Ciguralova, 2005; 2002; Mori, 2000; Portes & Madelon, 2001; Quatroche, 2000; Sakurako, 2000; Samovar, Porter & Stephani, 2000; Selmer, 2002; Tatar & Horenczyck, 2003; Tseng & Newton, 2002; Ward & Kennedy, 2001).

Bahvala (2002) shared common characteristics and challenges that foreign-born students face in their transition process to a new environment irrespective of their various psychological, cultural, social and academic backgrounds. In effect he recommended the need for their continued adjustment to a variety of cultural, academic, social, and linguistic differences. At this juncture it would be useful to observe that the transition process mentioned above presumes migration or mobility from one country, culture, and environment to another. It also entails duration and time factor in adjustment depending on each individual student's expectations, experiences, and perceptions of persons, issues, and things in a new culture and environment. Why do some adjustments take longer duration and process than they are presumed or expected to take? More research and scholarship that transcends the "how" of FBSs' migration as well as the mobility aspects of their lives and adjustment at colleges and universities is indeed, needed. This type of research will help to deeply probe into the why question above and come up with some solutions to the challenges in the FBSs' adjustment process. Understanding the reasons behind these challenges will help the researcher come to an appreciation of how to better serve FBSs as they navigate the complexities that may be involved in their college adjustment as much as boost their expectations. It is therefore this question of why, in connection with the difficulties and duration in FBSs' adjustment on campus that lead me to explore the FBSs' potential post-migration psycho-cultural adjustment challenges at community colleges. This project adopts the term psycho-cultural factors, in the above related sense. This study specifically explores family attachment, psychological disorientation, cultural inflexibility, home nostalgia, academic maladjustment, and identity consciousness as the natural, logical, and dynamic offshoots of the following major psycho-cultural components: ethnocentrism, stereotypes, prejudice, individualism, universalism and achievement; collectivism, particularism, and ascription (Adler, 2002; Belozersky, 1990; Blair-Brocker & Ernst, 2003; Erskine, 2002; Frost, 2002; Hazen & Alberts, 2006; Kim & Gudykunst, 1992; Kosic, 2002; Linklater, 2007; Lumby, 2006; Neuliep, 2008; Quatroche, 2000; Samovar, Porter & Stephani, 2000; Selmer, 2002; Smith, Dungan & Trompenaars, 1996; Trompenaars & Hampden-Turner, 1998; Wade and Travis, 2000; Ward & Kennedy, 2001; Ward & Ran-Deuba, 1999; Zakaria, 2000).

Basic Psycho-Cultural Adaptation Issues

Studies on cross-border adjustment intervention strategies have it that while awareness of what a cross-border manager is required to adjust to appears to be known, there appears to be less awareness of the more specific personal and behavioral strategies that are needed to assist adjustment. That is the extent to which interventions effectively address the personal wellbeing as a major psycho-cultural adaptability outcome of those who are required to adjust to a new culture and environment (Belozersky, 1990; Kosic, 2002; Ward & Kennedy, 2001; Ward & Ran-Deuba, 1999; Zakaria, 2000). The behavioral decisions made by cross-border managers have become key elements in understanding personal well-being and personal interaction necessary to assist effective adjustment.

Ward and Kennedy (2001) and Selmer (2002) in their reviews of adaptability and coping strategies among expatriates in Singapore and Hong Kong respectively provide support for this. They identified a variety of personal well-being (psycho-cultural adaptability outcome) difficulties such as depression that might manifest should some choose to pursue cultural avoidance behaviors. These avoidance behaviors may have resulted from foreign-born students' inability or failure to modify their cross-cultural priorities in a bid to accommodate the demands of a different as well as new cultural environment. Another explanation suggests a certain type of inflexibility toward previously learned cultural and social values, assumptions, judgments, and routines. In support of these analyses, past literature recommended a compulsory separation of students, in general, from past associations to enable them to make the expected transition, socialization, and finally get integrated into the life of the college. This is further summarized in their ability to relinquish one cultural setting be it physical, intellectual, or social as a necessary condition for a subsequent incorporation into another cultural setting (Kalsner & Pistole, 2003; Krosteng, 1992; Mattanah, Hancock, & Brand, 2004; Tinto, 1993). Awareness of major psycho-cultural adjustment challenges among FBSs CCs may provide better assistance not only in understanding the more important intervention strategies, but also the structure of the interventions, in providing services to these complex adjustment challenges that FBSs face during their transition and stay in college.

In a study of the psycho-cultural adjustment challenges of Soviet Jewish immigrants in the United States, Belozersky (1990) presented a psycho-cultural frame of reference and family dynamics during their period of adjustment. She examined immigration with its accompanying feelings of uprootedness, vulnerability, and numerous losses. In this article, she explored the difficulties and problems of adjustment that Soviet Jews grappled with during their resettlement in America. Belozersky described various maladaptive patterns of behavior exhibited by these immigrants based on their past experiences in a totalitarian society. She revealed that for many Soviet Jews adjustment to the new society and culture takes the form of a spectrum of physical and emotional reactions. She detailed out common psycho-cultural characteristics of Soviet immigrants as follows: unrealistic expectations, sense of entitlement, loss of the sense of security, identity by status, over-dependency, perseverance, manipulative behavior, difficulty in establishing trusting relationships, strong reliance on family and friends, and ambivalence about Jewish identity (Belozersky,1990). She suggested that awareness of important psycho-cultural characteristics of Soviet Jews may be helpful in providing more effective services to this refugee group in dealing with difficult behaviors and in facilitating the process of adaptation.

Academic Maladjustment and Psychological Disorientation

Research conducted on people in the early stages of their academic adjustment following migration has demonstrated that certain psycho-cultural factors influence students' school progress especially in math and reading (Quatroche, 2000). Quatroche found that with increased interest to prevent reading problems among school children, certain psycho-cultural variables, such as ethnic differences, early age reading, language literacy, environments of the home, and mathematics achievement have been noted to have an expanding literature that often point to the role of specific psycho-cultural factors. These factors have also been found to influence immigrant adolescents' adaptation to school. Portes and Madelon's (2001) study, which was focused on differential predictors of mathematics and reading among 5,267 second-generation immigrants in grades 8 and 9 in Miami, Florida and San Diego, California, support the preceding assertion. The result from two regression analyses, suggest some differences among psycho-cultural and ethno-cultural group predictors for reading and mathematics which are of both practical and statistical significance. More significantly, study indicated that these differences are dependent, to a large extent, on both psycho-cultural and demographic variables. However, it seems that the above research on the psycho-cultural influence focused research more on immigrant students in grades 8 and 9 than on foreign-born students or even immigrant students at community colleges. At least, the issues of the post-migration psycho-cultural factors have received less attention than they actually deserve. Therefore, this research paper is conceived as a major attempt to investigate potential post-migration psycho-cultural factors in their relationship with FBSs' adjustment at a community college especially from the perspective of possible FBSs' psychological, cultural, social, academic, and general psycho-cultural maladjustment.

Gudykunst and Kim (1997) pointed out that the psycho-cultural factors influencing communication with out-groups include stereotypes of and attitudes toward out-groups. They defined stereotypes as cognitive representations of another group that influence one's feelings about the group while arguing that stereotypes provide the content of social categories. In like manner, Samovar, Porter and Stephani (2000) refer to psycho-cultural factors as those culture-related ones in the domain of psychology. With concentration on the psycho-cultural factors, they explored their effects on communication effectiveness. There is a strikingly contextual proposition here that psycho-cultural factors often function as major barriers to intercultural communication and also points out ways to facilitate effectiveness. Interestingly, those psycho-cultural factors were adopted and classified as stereotypes, ethnocentrism, and prejudice.

According to Neuliep (2008), stereotyping is considered a type of attitudinal categorization which involves members of one group attributing characteristics to members of another group. These attributions typically carry either a positive or negative evaluation of members of a social group or class, such as sex, race, age, and profession as well as culture and nationality. Stereotyping can have negative impact on the members of the stereotyped groups; manifesting itself in the form of stereotype threat which is described as the fear or anxiety people feel when performing in some area in which their group is stereotyped to lack ability.

Focusing on the perception of group characteristics by outsiders, Wade and Travis (2000) defined stereotypes as the summary impression of a group of people in which a person believes that all members of a group share a common trait or traits. Holding a well-informed stereotype about a group of people (ethnic or cultural) may be helpful in interacting with individuals or members of the same group. However, if inaccurate stereotypes are tightly held about a group of people, they lead to inaccurate predictors of others' behaviors and even to miscommunication, breakdown in communication, or even misunderstanding. There is the possibility that this aspect of psycho-cultural challenges can trigger distrust or mistrust in various aspects of peoples' lives in relationship with others, in a new environment, and even in times of healthcare needs. Situations of prejudice and stereotypes may sometimes arise as a result of lack of trust such as when healthcare is sought.

Cheng (2004) conducted a study on foreign-born students' (international students') perceptions and experiences of using the university health system (UHS) at a public university in Northwest Ohio. Based on the focus group discussions, five themes emerged as the problems those students experienced including distrust in American health care. FBSs were said to have entertained misgivings about doctors telling them all the relevant aspects of prescription medications yet they (FBSs) did not have enough courage to question the medical professionals. This state of affairs left most students with the option of not going to the health center but instead to endure their symptoms until they visited their home country during breaks (Cheng, 2004). Not much is known about FBSs' trust in the US health care system as only qualitative studies with convenient samples have been conducted to address the problem. There remain questions of how much trust FBSs have in the US health system, which factors influence that trust, and how much cultural inflexibility as an offshoot of ethnocentrism is involved in this mentioned trust or mistrust.

In a cross-cultural adaptation and integrative theory Kim (2002) argued that a human being is a system who when confronted with a new culture, experiences inevitable disequilibrium. She notes that the impacted individual then incorporates feedback to bring the system back into balance. This theory carries with it the idea that a human person is the system who seeks to maintain balance. Interestingly, it is change in the environment that leads to disequilibrium or lack of balance. Her stress-adaptation-growth model suggests that adaptation is cyclical; two-steps-forward-one-step-back that she implies creates a drawback to leap. This theory which explores culture shock as either the ancestor or as an offshoot of psychological disorientation is portrayed in a different light as a good and necessary experience that leads to change, intercultural transformation, and personal growth. Kim anticipated the summary of her system's approach with the idea that by adjusting to a new culture we learn a new repertoire of thoughts, feelings, and behaviors. She sees cross-cultural mobility as empowering because its transformational impact through communication makes the migrant a different person and in a way a more multicultural, global, and a more complete person or a person with more choices. What makes this model unique and distinct from other models in the study of cross-culturalism is that in addition to communication with the host culture to which almost all theoretical models of foreign-born students' adjustment admit, Kim also believes that communication with people from the home culture, host receptivity, conformity pressure, and environmental influence can make adjustment easier and psychologically pleasant. But how do we explain a situation where a group of people from a given culture make assiduous efforts to achieve a healthy adjustment by learning and following the rules, norms, and values of a given culture but still feel miserable and sad? This question might have exposed the major limitations of this socio-cultural model which the psycho-cultural model seeks to supply in this present study.

Cultural Inflexibility and Identity Consciousness

Ethnocentrism has been described as a psycho-cultural characteristic that shows up in various forms like cultural inflexibility (cultural intolerance) and identity consciousness or identity confusion. These characteristics among others have been described as a tendency to see one's cultural norms, values, and ways of life as not only reasonable and proper but also innately superior to those of others (Samovar, Porter, & Stephani, 2000). Ethnocentrism could sometimes become controversial and deceptive because members of a given culture perceive and accept their own behavior as logical, reasonable, and of absolute value especially when that behavior at issue pays off. Ethnocentrism is universal although it changes in form and intensity across cultures. It carries some expectation from other people to follow one's ways of thinking, belief, and behavior. It comes with the tendency to interpret and evaluate out-groups' behavior using one's own standards. On a positive note ethnocentrism could be a protective mechanism that aims at reassuring the group and giving it a sense of purpose. To that end it tends to boost the morale of the group by extolling the qualities of its culture. Ethnocentric feelings also comprise a groups' urge to watch over and protect their own group against unfamiliar outsiders. One fact that is crystal clear is that many ethnic groups appreciate hospitality and peaceful relationships with other groups; however, when ethnocentrism becomes extreme and inflexible it may impair the groups' chances of survival (Samovar, Porter & Stephani, 2000).

Ethnocentric tendencies, which potentially breed cultural inflexibility, intolerance, and identity consciousness, can hinder people from learning about other cultures that can be found in various nations, states, cities, institutions, and schools especially when interacting with others. A solution to this challenge is proposed and summarized in flexible ethnocentrism suggested by Blair-Brocker and Ernst (2003). They suggested that people learn to accept that all of us are ethnocentric and realize that our cultural filters can distort reality. They further offered that we should recognize and appreciate that other people produce their own distortions of reality and learn to deal with issues resulting from ethnocentrism without emotions and judgments.

Ethnocentrism is often associated with prejudice which could be described as the judgment and decisions people make about persons, things, events, or situations based on their self-conception, belief system, previous experiences, perceptions, and assumptions. In relationships with other people, those who have unhealthy and perhaps inordinate levels of prejudice prefer to interact with those who are similar to them because such interactions are more comfortable and less stressful than interactions with out-groups. Individuals appear to learn prejudice against out-group members through family socialization processes, education, peer groups, mass media, and other influences (Plotnik, 2002). Prejudice tends to lead to stereotypes (or vice versa), which can be described as having a certain preconception about a particular group of people to the point of categorization or generalization about the group's identity without any attempt to perceive individual differences among the group members.

Samovar, Porter, and Stephani (2000) also admitted that on the one hand, ethnocentrism has positive effects that are often a source of cultural and personal identity. On the other hand, ethnocentrism in the form of identity crisis, identity confusion, or identity consciousness (IC), takes on a negative connotation and becomes destructive when it is used to shut others out, provide the bases for derogatory evaluation, and rebuff changes. This type of disposition may create a tendency where people become narrow-minded and even defensive about their sense of self and group identity. This ethnocentric proclivity is usually found in previously acquired as well as established forms of beliefs, attitudes, values, perceptions, assumptions, norms, and self- conceptions. In the case of foreign-born students in community colleges it will become both an internal and external struggle for them to strike equilibrium between their own inherited cultural elements and the social norms in their new environment as well as country of sojourn. Situations such as this could become sources of psychological adjustment difficulties showing up as frustrations, anxieties, stress, and even depression in FBSs' adjustment to various aspects of their college life and well-being. Psychological difficulties such as those enumerated find source in FBSs' perceptions, thoughts, and feelings may consequently be summarized in their various attitudes, opinions and behaviors in a new culture and environment.

One line of research picturing migrants' acculturation as challenging suggested a strong link between cross-cultural maladaptation and identity consciousness which is a psycho-cultural maladjustment indicator in this current research. Neuliep (2006), following the culture shock paradigm and its four-stage model, presented in Oberg (1960), examined the concept of acculturation in relation to immigrant groups. His discussion provides great and useful detail though some scholars might object to his views, which suggests that some migrants who do not adapt or acculturate are adopting maladaptive attitudes. These maladaptive patterns could be logically and most probably predicated on cultural inflexibility and identity consciousness as well as expressive in a circumstantial variable of psychological disorientation. These maladaptive patterns of behavior or attitudes could find better explanations and more nuanced analyses in Belozersky's (1990) theories on the migrants' or immigrants' thoughts, perceptions, and behaviors that are probably deep-seated in their feelings of uprootedness, vulnerability, and numerous losses such as the sense of entitlement, security, identity by status, as well as in their tendency to become over-dependent (collectivism) as against being self-reliant and independent (individualism). Some cultures value individualism while some others value collectivism. The former cultural orientation encourages individuals to seek out their own identity, make their own decisions based on their own values, and eventually become responsible for themselves. Individualism emphasizes independence, freedom, self-reliance, and autonomy. In the latter cultural orientation (collectivism), identity is conferred on someone as a member of a group, extended family, clan, or other social organization. Collectivism emphasizes interdependence, group solidarity, and consensus (Anbari, Khilkhanova, Romanova, & Umpleby, 2004; Belozersky, 1990; Hofstede, 2000; Triandis, 2002; Trompenaars and Hampden-Turner; 1998). Contextually, in the collectivist culture, the contribution of an individual to an entire group is viewed as more valuable than his or her own singular decision. This cultural orientation may affect a foreign-born students' comfort level with independence, assertiveness, and individuation. One of the contrasting features between collectivism and individualism is that what is normally viewed as a friendly gesture or favor in a collectivist society could be easily considered a burden or inconvenience in an individualist society. Findings from the above literature suggest that FBSs from a collectivist culture often feel uncomfortable with speaking up, standing out, and asserting themselves and would most of the time support the status quo or just conform to avoid trouble.

Dependency as an aspect of collectivism (communitarianism) is found in the majority of the countries from where foreign-born students come and has been variously theorized as discouraging autonomy and initiative which constitute aspects of individualism (Belozersky, 1990; Brehm, Kassim & Fein, 2002; Conover, 2009; Heine et al., 2001; Hogg & Williams, 2000; Oyserman, Coon & Kemmelmier, 2002; Singelis, 2000; Swagler & Ellis, 2003; Toomey, 1999; Triandis, 2002). Besides, this value of dependence tends to encourage the overprotection of children as well as expects them to please their parents and guardians. Therefore, circumstances and situations that suggest individual responsibility and the necessity to make independent choices could become threatening to FBSs and immigrants at large as that might provoke in them filial and some kind of helpless clinging attitude both to their host nations and host nationals. These perceptively misaligned sorts of feelings may have been based on the immigrants' previously assimilated misconceptions as well as the extremely idealized views of immigration and resettlement they held about their host country (Belozersky, 1990). Such feelings, perceptions, thoughts, and behaviors, when adopted by FBSs, could act as powerful stressors during the process of acculturation. For Neuliep (2008), this concept of acculturation that he observed some migrants to resist implies assimilation rather than a mere psychological comfort contrary to which immigrant groups would seek to hold on to aspects of their own identity while fully embracing American identity. Consistent with Neuliep's (2008) conceptual analysis on acculturation, Martin, Nakayama and Flores (2002) presented the works of other authors who observed that Asian immigrants practically refused to accept assimilation in an attempt to maintain some aspects of their culture of origin. These suggestions could be allowed to inform more specific questions, such as: is cultural adjustment dialectical; that is, existing in a dual tension or conflict? Is acculturation (cultural adjustment) total or is it fractured? Why do people adjust to a culture in some ways but deliberately maintain some elements of their original identity in other ways? Does there exist the possibility of adjusting psychologically (being very happy and comfortable) but not adjust in terms of adopting the norms of the new culture? This present psycho-cultural inquiry is certainly driven by a commitment to examine the possible relationship of this type of bicultural conflict in adjustment influenced by identity consciousness among FBS migrants.

In order to better explain cross-cultural differences as well as their implications for managing international and multicultural projects, Anbari, Khilkhanova, Romanova, and Umpleby (2004), theorized that cultural differences can interfere with the successful completion of projects in today's multicultural global business community. They described the most well-known and accepted cross-cultural management theories with the conclusion that global project management can only succeed through culturally-aware leadership, cross cultural communication, and mutual respect. The following questions remain unaddressed: How could an appropriate cross-cultural communication be established as well as mutual respect achieved without a profound understanding the bases of a people's cross-cultural values, attitudes, and behaviors that are strongly predicated on the psycho-cultural? In order to address this question, various theories were proposed as well as studies conducted.

Among the leading studies conducted on cross-cultural management, with psycho-cultural underpinnings, Hofstede (2000) advanced a set of deep cultural dimensions along which preponderant value systems could be aligned. Such cultural dimensions influence human thoughts, feelings, and behaviors as well as those of organizations and institutions in predictable forms. He theorized that sets of those cultural dimensions mirror fundamental problems that any society has to contend with but for which solutions vary. Hofstede found that similarities and differences among those problems exist in some respects. He identified differences between individualism and collectivism (communitarianism) as its opposite regarding the degree to which individuals are prone to look after themselves or simply maintain integration through groups, especially in the family. Hofstede also specifically defined individualism as a societal value where ties between individuals are loose. In this type of society everyone is supposed to look after himself or herself and his or her immediate family only. On the other hand, collectivism is defined as a cultural orientation where people from birth onward are integrated into strong, closely knit groups that provide them with life-long protection in exchange for some unequivocal allegiance. This study found the highest individualism in the United States, Australia, and the United Kingdom while the lowest individualism scores were found in Guatemala, Ecuador, and Panama.

In another cross-cultural study with profound psycho-cultural implications Trompenaars and Hampden-Turner (1998) provided another significant dimension of culture: universalism and particularism. Following the result of a survey conducted with about 28 countries, they found universalism to have a strong association with nations that place much emphasis on rules, laws, and regulations and go as far as applying them to all situations in contrast to the particularistic cultural dimension where members of a given society place more emphasis on relationships with the tendency to treat each situation differently. They argue that people from universalist societies put rules and regulations before relationships whereas those from particularistic societies might have the tendency to bend the rules and regulations in order to protect their friends and family members. To further delineate conflicts existing between the two orientations, previous research by Trompenaars and Hampden-Turner (1997) made these observations:

> A universalist would say this about particularists: "They cannot be trusted because they will always help their friends." Conversely, a

particularist would say this about universalists: "You cannot trust them as they would not even help a friend" (pp. 31-32).

A major point of contention in the above literature review would find universalists perceive those that identify with particularism as potentially corrupt, untrustworthy, unpredictable, and perhaps associated with nepotism. On the other hand, particularists would perceive universalists as cold, legalistic, inflexible, disloyal, and ridiculously wanting as team-players. Countries found to have scored highly in valuing universalism include Switzerland, United States, Canada, Australia, Netherlands, and Germany while countries like China, Russia, India, Korea, Nepal, Mexico, Japan, and other countries in Africa and South America are found to be more inclined toward particularism (Erskine, 2002; Frost, 2002; Linklater, 2007; Lumby, 2006; Smith, Dungan & Trompenaars, 1996; Trompenaars & Hampden-Turner, 1997).

Other studies (Hofstede, 2000; Trompenaars & Hampden-Turner, 1998) found that both achievement-oriented and ascription-oriented cultures distribute honors, status, power, and authority in different ways. In achievement-oriented societies effectiveness is determined as well as measured by action. The major focus of this cultural orientation is on doing and on respect hinged on knowledge, skill, and performance. Conferment of status is based upon each member's accomplishment. In such societies, status is used only when considered relevant depending on the competence and previous achievement of the individual involved. In preferring to do something over doing nothing, achievement cultures are considered to be action-oriented. On the other hand, the ascription-oriented cultures accord status based upon someone's social standing, age, gender, affluence, seniority, and similar factors. They value understanding the complexities of a given situation better before taking action. This cultural orientation focuses more on being, respect for age, status, hierarchy, and support for extensive use of titles. For them action should never be done in a hurry but rather should wait for the right time to act. This particular type of orientation can certainly affect the way foreign-born students relate to their host nationals. Most FBSs in the US are from cultures where honor, status, and respect are accorded without using personal achievement as the main criterion. This can be especially difficult as well as threatening to FBSs whose status may have been displaced in the US as result of this major difference in psycho-cultural orientations (Belozersky, 1990). This study further noted that countries that were found to be typically achievement-oriented include the US, Britain, Mexico and Germany while China, Russia, Japan, and Spain were considered ascription-oriented.

Family Attachment and Home Nostalgia

Family influence, reliance, and attachment have been extensively reported as profoundly impacting foreign-born students' adjustment and their further studies' decision making process (Constantine, Kindaichi, Okazaki, Gainor, & Baden 2005; Lawley, 1993; Mazzarol & Souter, 2002; Pimpa, 2003). Some of these studies mentioned only two aspects of family influence: recommendations and financial support. Among these studies none endeavored to clearly demonstrate how and why families exert influence on FBSs' adjustment behaviors or explain whether or not family influence exploring cultural adjustment experiences of 15 Asian, Indian, Japanese, Korean, and Vietnamese international college women through semi-structured discussions, Constantine, Kindaichi, Okazaki, Gainor, and Baden (2005) noted that FBS participants were generally excited about the academic and personal opportunities offered in the United States. However, they also typically indicated that they experienced sadness about leaving their homes for the US. One typically related subcategory stemmed from missing family, friends, and food from home. Some participants indicated they felt anxious about living in a foreign land. In order to cope with cultural adjustment problems, participants reported that they sought advice from family members when they experienced cultural adjustment problems.

Some strands of research on college students' adjustment in general versus familial relationships maintain that family connections impact students' initial transitions into college as well as their continued college experiences (Wartman & Savage, 2008; Wintre & Yaffe, 2000). Other studies that are psychologically based not only focused primarily on the first two years in college but also linked family relationships to the college transition process. They examined students' ability to individuate or separate themselves from their parents. On a different note, they assumed that this ability to individuate as predictive of a student's successful transition into college as well as to his or her sense of belonging on campus in the coming years (Kalsner & Pistole, 2003; Mattanah, Hancock & Brand, 2004). This study and its findings seem to be more appropriate for students from individualistic cultures as opposed to foreign-born students that mostly belong to collectivist cultures.

Previous studies on foreign-born students' adjustment challenges in college have been associated with feelings of homesickness, loneliness, insufficient social support, as well as relationship difficulties found that approximately 78 % of FBSs reported experiencing feelings of loneliness whenever they thought about friends and family not being physically present with them in the US (Chavajay & Skowronek, 2008; Misra, Crist & Durant, 2003; Poyrazli, Arbona, Nora, McPherson, & Pisecco, 2004; Wang & Mallinckrodt, 2006). Misra, Crist and Durant (2003) examined the impact of social support from family and friends on academic stressors among 143 FBSs at two universities in the Midwest. They concluded that greater social support predicted lower scores for reactions to stressors. They also found that FBSs' contact with family and friends from their home countries and with other FBSs provided the greatest source of socials support and were significantly helpful in reducing academic stressors and their resultant effects.

The major target of a psycho-cultural investigation in this project is therefore to logically bridge that conceptual crossroad in human development and relationships, where assimilated complex cultural systems and values meet human psychology. Because of this vitalizing interplay between the psychological and cultural as essential components (underpins) of this psycho-cultural concept, further literature review on the psychological and cultural adjustment will subsequently be conducted with a view to sharpening the edge of the product of these two major aforementioned psycho-cultural underpins: the psychological and the cultural.

Psychological Adjustment

While Mori (2000) suggested that foreign-born students in American colleges represent a diverse and constantly growing population their unique concerns are traditionally believed to have been over-looked. Among these concerns include the demands for cultural adjustments that frequently place FBSs at greater risk for various psychological problems than students in general necessitating sufficient and readily accessible mental health services. A longitudinal survey was conducted on 294 international and domestic student sojourners to examine and compare their adjustment and distress or strain responses during the first six months of their entry into a medium-sized, mid-western US state university (Hechanova-Alampay, Beehr, Christiansen & Van Horn, 2002). The findings revealed that FBSs compared to domestic students had greater difficulty during their initial transition into the university. Even though sojourners experienced increasing adjustment challenges overtime, the pattern of strain was curvilinear, peaking three months after the start of the semester. Self-efficacy, social support, and cultural novelty predicted adjustment and strain at different times during the transition period (Hechanova-Alampay, Beehr, Christiansen & Van Horn, 2002).

The adjustment challenges faced by foreign-born students have also been described as mostly psychological in nature. Consistent with this assertion, Tseng and Newton (2002) suggested with detailed illustration that FBSs must adjust through a process of psychological transition. The length of the process depends on the individual student's condition, including proficiency in English language, previous experience in cultural adjustment, support system, and general self-efficacy. Aside from exploring FBSs' strategies and coping skills at maintaining and sustaining well-being during their study abroad adjustment experience, this literature seems to have also given us in-depth information on what constitutes the FBSs' psychological challenges as a major part of the foundation of this study. However, their assertion that qualitative inquiry alone constitutes the preferred method for gaining a complete and detailed understanding of FBSs' experiences may have left something missing. This study employs a primarily qualitative design of grounded theory to investigate FBSs' understanding of well-being and to explore their strategies for maintaining as well as sustaining their own well-being while studying abroad. Two FBSs were interviewed to obtain their perception of their sources of well-being during their study abroad experience. It is unlikely that the conclusion will hold across any target population. Therefore, data on generalization to many other FBSs that were not interviewed will definitely be lacking. Grounded theory utilizes only a descriptive, interpretive approach through a more naturalistic inquiry that does not involve hypothesis testing in the conventional model. Data are only generated based on participants' views rather than using an existing theory or purely empirical method. The method of analysis involved in this type of study increased levels of abstraction involving the researchers' use of constant comparative procedures and asking questions from participants about their data. It therefore focuses on the subjective meanings provided by participants based on their own understanding of the interview questions posited, explicit researcher values, and beliefs suggestive of tentative conclusions (Charmaz, 2000; Creswell, 2002). For this current investigative study, I focused on identifying the potential psycho-cultural factors that impact FBSs' adjustment at community colleges using an empirically verifiable strategy. This strategy helps to illustrate and illuminate the issue of psycho-cultural adjustment challenges among FBSs at the selected community college that has been largely ignored in the previous research.

In a bid to determine the prevalence of mental health needs, awareness and use of counseling services by international graduate students, Hyun, Quinn, Madon, & Lustig (2007) surveyed 3,121 students out of which 551 were international graduate students. Approximately 44 percent of international graduate students responded that they had had an emotional or stress-related problem in the past year. The overall result indicated that there were some unmet mental health needs among international graduate students that could negatively affect their general academic progress and well-being. The gap left unfilled in this study has therefore been compensated for in this study on the psycho-cultural adjustment challenges of foreign-born students in community colleges. Often surveys about the mental concerns of FBSs are conducted among the students in the classrooms or student organizations. However less is known about those who use counseling services or why many seldom seek counseling services. No doubt, the above study contributed to the body of knowledge regarding the mental health needs of FBSs in several ways. However, more studies that utilize data from FBSs who may have actually availed themselves of campus counseling services especially in CCs have been employed in this research on the psycho-cultural adjustment challenges of FBSs at community colleges in the Northeastern US. This psycho-cultural study includes subgroup differences in each cluster of adjustment and goes a long way into a deeply investigative study by eliciting more information than was previously obtained.

Cultural Adjustment

A review of literature on cultural adjustment suggests that a period of acculturation is inevitable for foreign-born students. They will likely experience culture shock, loneliness, social isolation, and homesickness. They may be burdened with financial concerns that are more complex than usually experienced by domestic students because of differences in their cultural values and special meaning they may be assigning to those concerns. Moreover, FBSs are often targets of perceived bias or blatant racial discrimination (Chen, 1999; Nilsson, Berkel, Flores, & Lucas, 2004; Rajapaksa & Dundes, 2003; Schmitt, Spears & Branscombe, 2003).

Ward, Bochner, and Furnham (2001) asserted that coping with culture shock can positively impact foreign-born students if they are encouraged to adapt and synthesize cultural experiences in a positive way. However, culture shock is an inevitable process that all FBSs undergo in their efforts to adjust to a new culture. This inevitability has some psycho-cultural underpinnings thereby making these types of feelings unavoidable for FBSs because their well-being is under threat. Conceptualizing culture shock, which details emotional changes in intercultural adjustment over time, takes us back to the anthropologist Oberg's (1960) description of the successful sojourner who progresses through four stages of the same phenomenon. The first stage consists of the honeymoon phase where all encounters in the new environment are seen as exciting, positive, and stimulating. This may last from a few days or weeks to six months, depending on circumstances. The second stage is the crisis phase characterized by a hostile and aggressive attitude towards the host country. This hostility evidently grows out of the genuine difficulty experienced by the visitor in the process of adjustment; a feeling of disorientation and not knowing what is going on. The third stage is the recovery phase that starts with the visitor accepting the fact that there is a problem that needs to be addressed. It comes in the form of a compromise between the feeling and thinking of the honeymoon phase and the crisis phase. The fourth and final stage is the adjustment phase when the visitor is able to work effectively, know the limitations of their skills and can take on new ways of doing things and, most importantly, able to be more flexible. It is a stage when adjustment is about as complete as it can be with the visitor accepting the customs of the country as just another way of living (Marx, 2001; Oberg, 1960; Ward, Bochner, & Furnham, 2001) Some researchers have extended this concept to various stages with the conviction that adjustment as a major stressful life event, a view that has been shared by many investigators. The contributions of these researchers on culture shock make an explicit distinction between the affective, cognitive, and behavioral responses to cross-cultural contacts that they suggest lead to two distinct outcomes: psychologically and socio-culturally positive self-enhancement and assimilation. These outcomes uphold overriding positive criterion (dependent) variables of inter-cultural or cross-cultural contact (Hofstede, Hofstede, & Minkov, 2010; Pedersen, 1995; Ward, Bochner & Furnham, 2001).

Culture shock is believed to be precipitated by the anxiety that results from losing all familiar signs and symbols of social intercourse. Interestingly, Oberg (1960) argues that when Americans or other foreigners in a strange land get together to grouse about host country and its people-one can be sure they are suffering from culture shock. Culture shock, as a potential offshoot of psycho-cultural maladjustment propensity, potentially triggered by psychological disorientation, happens inside each individual who encounters unfamiliar events and unexpected circumstances. As the situation changes in unexpected directions, the individual needs to construct new perspectives on self, others, and the environment that fit with the new situation. It is defined as an internalized construct or perspective developed in reaction or response to the new or unfamiliar situation (Marx, 2001; Pedersen, 1995; Ward, Bochner & Furnham, 2001).

Understandably, each stage of culture shock might psychologically or emotionally affect students' behavior, yet students respond to each of those stages in various ways. This assertion is implicated in the conceptualization of cultural adjustment that is very much contingent upon the level of disposition and comprehension of different personalities as well as the extent of their ability to respond to new cultures and different perspectives (Ward, Bochner & Furnham, 2001). Hence the need for a mixed-method study anchored on a cross-sectional survey exercise and a focus group research approach of a psycho-cultural dimension. In the study of foreign-born students' adjustment challenges, at a midsize community college in northeastern US, it is critical to establish possible culture shock experiences by first exploring potential predictor variables from an exclusively psycho-cultural angle. This type of study will also help, in some ways, to envisage to a significant extent how to minimize the adverse effects of culture shock as well as maximize the positive outcomes of cross-cultural contacts involving FBSs at CCs.

Some researchers have also worked on a combination of challenges such as the socio-cultural adjustment issues and challenges of foreign-born students at four-year colleges and universities (Gloria & Ho, 2003; Stromquist & Monk man, 2000; Tomich, McWhirter, & Darcy, 2003, Toyokawa & Toyokawa, 2002; Tseng & Newton, 2002). However, these studies stopped short of studying FBSs' adjustment challenges from a psycho-cultural perspective which has more to do with the confluence of acquired and shared values, attitudes, norms, beliefs, and convictions as well as myths and legends that influence one's thoughts, feelings and actions. These are summarized in the larger issue of self or group identity or in the presentation of oneself or group within a new environment and culture. It often finds expression in the special and frequently unconventional meanings that individuals and groups assign to issues, events, and things (Adler, 2002; Ross, 2001).

Khoo, Abu-Rasain and Hornby (2002) describe cultural adjustment as a psychological process that focuses on the attitudinal and emotional adjustment of the individual to the new environment. This description once more delineates the depth as well as the nature of intricate connectivity existing between these two but complementary elements of culture and psychology. This study further stated that foreign-born students face numerous, and varied challenges, most of which show up as they try to adjust to new cultures and environments. The details of the problems that they experience as outlined in this study could be summarized from a psycho-cultural viewpoint even though there was no such direct reference. These problems usually and expectedly become barriers in their overall progress unless strategically and adequately addressed.

Psycho-cultural Adjustment Challenges and Student Outcomes
A. Academic Engagement/Achievement

Studies have also been conducted on the academic, linguistic, social, and cultural adjustment challenges of foreign-born students at four-year colleges and universities (Burrell & Kim, 2002; Chen, 1999; Ciguralova, 2005; Crawford, 2000; Leslow-Hurley, 2000; Sakurako, 2000; Wang & Frank, 2002; Yi, Lin & Kishimoto, 2003). For instance,

Yi, Lin, and Kishimoto found that FBSs who experienced high achievement in their home countries were particularly prone to suffer negative psychological feelings (anxieties) in connection to their academic achievements. They examined subgroup differences among FBSs relating to demographic factors, reasons for seeking counseling, referral sources, and self-reported concerns. Academic anxiety and depression were major concerns for FBSs in their study. Undergraduates were reported to worry more about their grades than graduate students did; however graduate students were more likely to report relationship problems with a romantic partner. The results also revealed that gender, age, and grade point average (GPA) were related to reasons for seeking counseling. Because of differences in the system of education and teaching methodologies, FBSs may experience a high discrepancy between their expected and actual academic performance and this can create high levels of anxiety for them (Chen, 1999). Examining their expectations in this regard took me to a psycho-cultural study directed to determine whether or not FBSs have distinctively hereditary academic traditions and delineate how FBSs perceive things in their academic lives and involvements, interpret them, as well react to academic environments that are relatively new to them. It may also reveal possible academic maladjustment arising from a certain shift from their previous experiences in classroom learning and teaching methodologies as well as certain academic idiosyncrasies in their countries of origin to a given system that is probably novel. Student outcome with academic engagement or performance resulting from psycho-cultural adjustment challenges is largely ignored in the existing research. Therefore, this investigation attempts to explore those outcomes among groups and subgroups of FBSs at CCs in northeastern US.

B. Social Interaction and General Well-Being Issues

Miscellaneous challenges that foreign-born students face with residential transition, counseling and health services, housing, tuition costs, immigration and documentation, safety threats, and dietary issues have also been highlighted in some studies (Berkner, He, Lew, Cominole, Siegel & Griffith,2005; Sam, 2001, Yang, Wong, Hwang, & Heppner), while fewer studies have examined adjustment challenges of FBSs either at community colleges or at four-year colleges (Brickman & Nuzzo, 1999; Chen, 1999, Dozier, 2001; Lamkin, 2000). In an attempt to understand FBSs at CCs more, some researchers (Kisell, 2007; Lamkin, 2000; Stroman, 2004) examined their experiences, perceptions, and performances in CCs with two studies focusing only on a special group of international in the English as a second language (ESL) program. Other researchers (Brewer, 2005; Chen, 2003; Cohen, 2007; Doku, 2007; Zeszotarski, 2003) studied FBSs' adjustment experiences in CCs that include the ESL students' experiences, technology use, and traditional academic experiences of FBSs at CCs. Cohen (2007) specifically described 26 challenges and barriers facing FBSs at CCs. Among these barriers were stress, family, and finances in a new cultural climate, the rigors of learning English language, disrespect from faculty, staff, and American students as well as lack of information of community college procedures and services.

Lee and Rice (2007) conducted a study that explored the experiences of foreign-born students at a research university in the

Southwestern US. This research documented a range of difficulties that FBSs face ranging from perceptions of unfairness and inhospitality to cultural intolerance and confrontation. Neo-racism, which has to do with discrimination on the basis of cultural or national superiority and an increasing rationale for marginalizing or assimilating groups in a globalizing world, was used as a framework to explain many of their experiences. The analysis and discussions were organized around their words and the contexts in which the difficulties they encountered emerged. At this juncture it therefore stands to reason that not all the challenges that FBSs face can be classified as issues of adjustment but that some of those difficulties come from the societies that occupy the positions of host countries to them (Lee & Rice, 2007).

Although the focus of most studies has been more on academic, social, cultural, or psychological issues, there is lack of research on the social or interactional student outcome of post-migration psycho-cultural adjustment challenges among foreign-born students in community colleges as several pointed out. Research, on the psycho-cultural adjustment challenges that FBSs face reveals their values, assumptions, beliefs, convictions, and attitudes, as well as their perceptions on these issues. It also reveals the impact of these psycho-cultural factors on student adjustment outcome with socialization and interaction on campus as well as their general well-being. Without this type of study, higher education in the United States may remain unfamiliar with this unique population of students and perhaps leave a wide gap in "the specifically designed programs that might be needed to meet their unique needs" (Upcraft, Gardner, Barefoot, & Associates, 2005, p.441).

College counselors, certainly, need to modify traditional theories and techniques to suit particular needs and unique concerns of their foreign-born students. A psycho-cultural examination of the post-migration adjustment challenges of FBSs makes an important difference. Contrary to other studies on academic, social, cultural, or psychological difficulties of FBSs, it explores the depth and intensity of adjustment challenges of FBSs at CCs from the dimension of disposition, perceptions of the external world and even motives for individual and group representation (Ross, 2001). To give this issue a clearer illustration, psychology and counseling theories have, traditionally, included culturally specific assumptions based on universal definitions of what constitutes normal behavior in such a way that they typically favor individualism as an aspect of culture over the ideals of collectivism as another aspect of culture. Because of the diverse nature of these students' college counseling services, problem-solving and conflict resolution programs may be restructured to include alternative forms of formative and counseling approaches, incorporating psycho-cultural and psycho-educational educational programs (Komiya & Eells, 2001; Sadeghi, Fisher & House, 2003).

Summary and Evaluation

Indeed, the aforementioned literature shows that foreign-born students from various countries and continents across the globe arrive into the United States mostly for further studies. Related theories, concepts, and research also testify to the fact that these groups of students certainly experience some adjustment challenges that have been variously classified as psychological, cultural, academic, and social as well as other miscellaneous challenges (Bahvala, 2002; Barletta & Kobayashi, 2007; Burrell & Kim, 2002; Chen, 1999; Ciguralova, 2005; Crawford, 2000; Leslow-Hurley, 2000; Sakurako, 2000; Wang & Frank, 2002; Yi, Lin, & Kishimoto, 2003). Other research in this field takes a moderate approach that stresses the function of cognition within a psychological context and examines the ways that people's thoughts affect how they feel, what they want, and how they respond to stimuli in their environment (Brehm, Kassim, & Fein, 2002). These pieces of research provide a basis to this study of potential post-migration psycho-cultural adjustment challenges that FBSs face in community colleges. This is due in part because a close link has been established between cultural orientation and conceptions of the self (psychological orientation) as students transition to a new culture and environment. These cultural orientations have been shown to impact the way people perceive, evaluate, and present themselves in relation to others as well as to their environments (Kroger, 2000; Kagitcibasi, 2005). This study of the post-migration psycho-cultural adjustment challenges facing FBSs is thus informed by both unique psychological and cultural orientations that are clearly lacking in some of the previously reviewed studies on FBSs' adjustment challenges at colleges and universities.

The preceding allusions to psychological and cultural orientations have indeed provided basis for this special vocabulary: *psycho-cultural*. Many potential post-migration psycho-cultural adjustment issues of foreign-born students at community colleges that are clearly lacking in previous and existing research remain to be examined by a new investigation. Therefore, the concentration of this study is solely given to the psycho-cultural element of FBSs' adjustment challenges. This perspective is the product of the integration of both the psychological and the cultural orientations linked to the bases of the behavioral process (Berger, 2001; Brehm, Kassim, & Fein, 2002; Kroger, 2000; Kagitcibasi, 2005). By employing this perspective, I felt better able to understand the inner workings of the behavior of interest among FBSs at participating CCs. The anticipated outcomes of this research may also help CCs redefine, restructure, and even refine their FBSs' orientation programs, academic curricula, teaching methods, counseling services, and methodology. It, therefore, behooves higher education to be involved in this type of research so that the theoretical aspects of FBSs' potential post-migration psycho-cultural adjustment challenges are accurately integrated and realized in this project.

CHAPTER III
Research Methodology

Introduction

This chapter discusses methods and procedures utilized in this research to examine psycho-cultural adjustment challenges (barriers) of foreign-born students at community colleges in the Northeastern United States. Detailed information about the research population, the instruments used, and the procedure by which data were collected and analyzed is included. This study is designed to add to the limited body of research in this area of foreign-born students' adjustment and to provide educators, policy-makers, administrators, counselors, and international student directors with the necessary information to make recommendations for policy, practice, and future research. The three main research questions answered by this study are:

1. To what extent and in what ways do FBSs enrolled in CCs in the US face post-migration psycho-cultural adjustment challenges?

2. To what extent and in what ways do post-migration psycho-cultural adjustment challenges differ among groups of FBSs (such as gender, age, year in college, continent of origin, marital status and family presence) enrolled in CCs in the US?

3. To what extent and in what ways are post-migration psycho-cultural adjustment challenges related to the outcomes (Social Interaction and Academic/Career Engagement) of FBSs' adjustment at CCs in the US?

Research procedure included a major pilot test and subsequent factor and reliability analyses. Participation for the pilot test was solicited from FBSs at eight CCs in the Northeastern United States. Information regarding pilot testing is contained in this chapter; further organized into the following subsections: Method and Design, Population and Study Sites, Sample, Instrumentation, Data Collection, Human Subjects' Protection and Data Analysis.

Method and Design

A mixed method approach integrating both quantitative and qualitative research methods was utilized in this study (Creswell, 2003; Gay & Airasian, 2003). This model was chosen because of a great deal of advocacy developed in favor of blending qualitative and quantitative methods as well as linking data given their non-oppositional empirical relationship (Creswell, 2003, Curlette, 2006). The combination of both approaches provides a more textured and productive view of the psycho-cultural phenomenon we seek to explore, sharpens understanding of research findings with evidence serving to strengthen the case of causality and generality (Krathwohl, 2004; Bryman, 2006).

This mixed methodological approach involved a single cross-sectional study design which employed an explanatory participant selection model. The explanatory participant selection model is used when a researcher needs quantitative information to identify and purposefully select participants for an in-depth qualitative study. In this model, the qualitative data were used to further explain the quantitative findings (Bryman, 2006; Creswell & Plano-Clark, 2007). This mixed method approach is therefore intended to gather enough information from foreign-born students at participating community colleges on their potential post-migration psycho-cultural adjustment challenges. In an explanatory design participant selection model, quantitative data collection is done at the beginning of the study. I used the quantitative information to identify and purposefully select participants, and generate and refine questions for the focus group session. This approach also provided the context for the qualitative analysis (Creswell, 2002; Krathwohl, 2004).

Population and Study Sites

Three participating community colleges are midsize and located in the suburban areas of the Northeastern United States. Two of these CCs are in the state of New Jersey while one is in the state of New York. There were a total of 1,650 foreign-born students enrolled for the 2011-2012 academic year in the three participating CCs. This population represents FBSs from approximately 61 countries across the globe. Among the CCs in the State of New Jersey, one has a population of 701 FBSs while the other has a population of 330 FBSs. The CC in the New York has a population of 619 FBSs. Survey participants were FBSs who were enrolled in the three selected CCs in Northeastern United States. Population for this study includes both female and male FBSs. Their academic programs at the time of this study included arts, science, applied science, business administration, health care, nursing, ESOL, ESL and liberal arts degree programs and certificate programs. About 75% of the entire student population in each CC is enrolled in non-credit professional development courses through the Division of Continuing Education. Like other CCs in the US, they prepare students for transfer to four year colleges and universities or for immediate entry into a career.

It is of interest to note that the participating community colleges have centers for intercultural learning and understanding one of which serves as a monument to revitalize a long-standing commitment to institutional diversity. Almost all these CCs have at least two counselors who provide services and programs for current foreign-born students at the International Student Centers. The counselors help them during their tenure at the CCs to understand how to maintain their immigration status. These CCs were chosen for research because of the relatively large population of their FBSs and because they offer the expected diversity that enabled me to arrive at a fairly reliable research result.

Sample

Survey sampling procedure and description

Participants consisted of foreign-born students from Africa, Asia, Latin America, Europe, Middle East, and North America. On the whole, the sample was a total of 382 FBSs. This sample incorporated all immigrant and non-immigrant students, all of whom are foreign-born. I undertook a convenience non-probability sampling technique because issues of central importance to research are explored from a particular and specified group (FBSs) regarding phenomenon of interest. This non-probability sampling technique sought to include all accessible (willing and available participants) FBSs in the classroom setting. Only obliging FBSs who responded to researcher's solicitation letter and were available in class on the days allotted for survey data collection by each CC were surveyed. The total respondents from the three CCs were used as sample in this study. Following is the abridged breakdown of the survey sample demographics:

Gender and age

Participants in the survey study comprised 69% (262) females and 31% (120) males. About 50% (190) of IS respondents were within the age range of 18-25. Approximately 30% (115) were within the age range of 26-35. Twelve percent (48) were within the age range of 36-45. Five percent (20) were within the age range of 46-55. About 1% (3) was within the age range of 56-65 while 2 % (6) were over 65.

Year in college and program of studies

Respondents who were in year one at the community colleges were 55% (211). Twenty six percent (97) were in year two while 19% (74) were over year two in college. At the time of the survey study, current or intended programs of studies of these respondents included arts, science, applied science, business administration, health care, nursing and liberal arts.

Marital and family presence status

Sixty-one percent (233) of the 382 respondents in this survey research were single. Thirty four percent (128) were married while 5% (21) were divorced. Sixty nine percent (264) indicated that they had families or relatives in the United States while 31% (118) remnants do not have families or relatives in the US.

Table 1

Respondents' Sample Represented by Continents below

Continent	Frequency	Percent
Asia	81	21%
Latin America	172	45%
Europe	85	22%
Africa	17	5%
Middle East	14	4%
North America	13	3%
Total	382	100%

Focus Group Participant Demographics

Participants were volunteer FBSs who were enrolled in the two (both in New Jersey) of the three selected CCs in Northeastern United States.

Table 2

Focus Group Participants' Demographics

Part.	Age	Continent	Marital Status	Yr. in College	Academic Program
#1	34	N. America	Married (F)*	2	Liberal Arts
#2	31	S. America	Married (F)	2	Nursing
#3	27	Asia	Single(F)	3	Health Science
#4	29	Asia	Single(F)	3	World Language Program
#5	28	N. America	Single(M)*	2	Business Administration
#6	21	S. America	Single(F)	1	Communic-ations Arts
#7	25	Europe	Single(F)	2	Biology
#8	28	S. America	Single(F)	2	Business Management
#9	27	Mid-East	Single(M)	3	Engineering
#10	28	S. America	Single(F)	3	International Studies

*(F) signifies Female participants while *(M) signifies Male participants

Gender and Age

Participants in this focus-group discussion session comprised 80% (8) females and 20% (2) males. The average age of the participants was 27.6 with the range of ages from 21 to 34.

Academic programs

Respondents who were enrolled in English as a second language program (ESL) were six (6), in number, while those preparing to enroll in the major university programs or enrolled already in the main college programs were four (4), in number. At the time of the focus group session, current or intended programs of studies of these participants included science, business administration, health care, nursing, and liberal arts.

Marital and family presence status

Eighty percent (8) of the ten participants in this study were single. Twenty percent (2) were married with children. Forty percent (4) indicated that they have families or relatives in the United States while 60% (6) others do not have families or relatives in the US.

Instrumentation

Psycho-Cultural Adjustment Survey

To quantify knowledge of the proposed phenomenon, I developed a 43-item Likert-type *Psycho-Cultural Adjustment Scale Questionnaire* (PCASQ), based on literature review, to utilize in this study (see Appendix A). In addition to demographic information, the questionnaire contains items that examine the criterion (dependent) variables of foreign-born students' adjustment (psychological, cultural, academic, and social adjustment) and predictor variables or factors predicting potential post-migration psycho-cultural maladjustment of FBSs at community colleges in the Northeastern US.

Demographic items requested information on age, gender, country of origin, continent and year in college. The survey was designed to cover four major areas of foreign-born students' adjustment at community colleges. These include psychological, cultural, academic and social components of adjustment. Aside from the demographic section, the questionnaire encapsulates items that examine major factors influencing

FBSs' psycho-cultural maladjustment. Those factors are comprised of identity consciousness and home nostalgia; psychological disorientation and cultural inflexibility; family attachment and academic maladjustment.

Relevant literature review shows that there are a variety of correlations of foreign-born students' psycho-cultural adjustment challenges that include post-migration and transitional factors (Sakurako, 2000; Samovar, Porter & Stephani, 2000; Selmer, 2001; Tatar & Horenczyck, 2003; Tseng & Newton, 2002;Wade & Travis, 2000; Ward & Kennedy, 2001). Family attachment, psychological disorientation, cultural inflexibility, home nostalgia, academic maladjustment, and identity consciousness, are among the most commonly touted and suspected antecedents (indicators) of FBSs' psycho-cultural adjustment challenges (Belozersky, 1990; Blair-Brocker & Ernst, 2000; Kim & Gudykunst, 1992; Kosic, 2002;Neuliep, 2008; Plotnik, 2002; Portes & Madelon, 2001; Quatroche,2000; Ross, 2001; Samovar, Porter & Stephani, 2000; Wade & Travis, 2000; Ward & Kennedy, 2001; Ward & Ran-Deuba, 1999; Zakaria, 2000).

Focus Group Discussion Guide Questions

To obtain data for the qualitative side of this study, a focus group session guide questions were developed (see Appendix B). Guide questions contains a total of 26 items intended to elicit information on foreign-born students' opinions, thoughts, and feelings on their potential post-migration psycho-cultural adjustment challenges at community colleges. Items comprise introductory questions, post-migration/transitional questions, key questions, outcome questions (academics and interactive), and wrap up questions (Krueger & Casey, 2000).

As a researcher, I primarily sought to learn about possible differences in perspectives between groups or categories of foreign-born students on their potential post-migration psycho-cultural adjustment challenges at community colleges. The purpose is to uncover factors that influence their thoughts, feelings, motivation and behavior, post migration, in a foreign land from their countries of birth. I expected ideas, themes, and patterns to emerge from the focus group session to supplement the quantitative data collected.

Survey and Interview Question-Guide Development

The survey instrument and the interview questions were developed based on six major constructs (psychological disorientation, cultural inflexibility, academic maladjustment, identity consciousness, home nostalgia, and family attachment) gleaned from the relevant literature review. These foundational (fundamental) constructs are intended to measure potential post-migration psycho-cultural adjustment challenges of foreign-born students at the participating community colleges. Experts in the fields of psychology and education examined these constructs which incorporated reviews, definitions, and questions for each construct. Several items were either modified or eliminated based on the discretion of experts in the subjects. This step of the survey and interview development was necessary to establish content validity.

After completing the surveys as well as reviewing the interview questions, a few foreign-born students were asked to comment on both instruments. Upon obtaining the Institutional Review Board's (IRB) approval, draft versions of the survey instrument and the interview (focus group session) schedule were pilot-tested with only participants from Seton Hall University's undergraduate school, mostly in the Department of International Studies. Feedback from the mock pilot-test was used to revise several survey items, clarify, and fine-tune questions. Several items that did not directly provide data pertaining to the research questions were also removed. Both instruments were sent to several scholars of higher education as well as faculty both at Seton Hall University and elsewhere. They provided commentary and suggestions on the structure of both the survey instrument and focus-group session protocols.

Using feedback from foreign-born students and experts in higher education, anthropology, psychology, sociology, and statistics, the survey was revised several for purposes of clarity. Remnant items that did not provide data pertaining to the research questions were finally removed. After the content validity of both the survey instrument and interview questions were established, the survey instrument had 36 items while the interview protocol had 23 questions.

Contributions of the Major Pilot Survey

Following the establishment of content validity upon the approval of proposal by the Seton Hall University Institutional Review Board (IRB) the main pilot survey utilizing the instrument was conducted to establish construct validity. The purpose of construct validity is to determine if the constructs being measured are a valid conceptualization of the phenomenon being tested (Wallen & Fraenkel, 2001). The survey was pilot tested with foreign-born students from community colleges and their equivalents in both New York and New Jersey and validated from July to

October, 2011. I used the feedback gleaned from these pilot tests to modify items on the survey instrument. Modifications were made to reflect potential post-migration psycho-cultural adjustment challenges of FBSs at US CCs.

Data from the pilot study were analyzed through the use of factor analysis to determine if indeed given items loaded on the intended constructs. Factor analysis is a technique that identifies and summarizes the many inter-relationships that exist among individual variables or factors. It identifies a small number of factors that may be used to represent relationships among sets of interrelated variables (George & Malley, 2000). During this process of factor analysis, items that did not load on the intended constructs were eliminated given their inadequacy to measure those constructs. Through factor analysis of data, the survey instrument was reduced from 39 to 36 items as 3 items had low factor loading that overlapped across all constructs indicating that they were not good measures of specific constructs. The final instrument included six items that measured psychological and environmental disorientation, five items that measured cultural inflexibility, three items that measured academic maladjustment, seven items that measured family attachment, five items that measured academic/campus maladjustment, six items that measured identity consciousness and two items that measured social interaction issues. Five items were eliminated because of low factor loadings.

Factor Correlations

Inspection of the correlation matrix, based on the original eight scales, indicates that the family attachment scale is positively related to psychological disorientation, cultural inflexibility, academic maladjustment, identity consciousness and home nostalgia scales. The psychological distress scale is positively correlated to family attachment, cultural inflexibility, and academic maladjustment scales. The cultural inflexibility scale is positively correlated to those of academic maladjustment and identity consciousness. Academic maladjustment is positively correlated rather highly to identity consciousness with 0.693. Identity consciousness is positively correlated to psychological disorientation, cultural inflexibility and academic maladjustment. Home nostalgia is positively correlated to the ethnocentrism scale. Ethnocentrism is positively correlated to cultural inflexibility and social interaction scales while the interaction scale is positively correlated to home nostalgia.

Scores for each scale were calculated by dividing the total items scores for each scale by the number of items in the scale. Coefficient alpha estimates for these scales were .81, .77, .70, .67, .67, .57, .58, and .59 from family attachment to identity consciousness scales, respectively.

Reliability and Validity of Scales

Table 3

Reliability Coefficients

Number of Cases (N) = 382

Number of Items (variables) (N) = 36

Alpha (Standardized items) = Alpha = 0. 844

Analyses of data from the pilot test determined the validity and reliability of the instrument as well as the Cronbach's alpha which is the internal consistency or reliability coefficient for an instrument requiring only one administration. The reliability and validity of the entire survey instrument were established and the Cronbach's alphas of the emerging factors (compound components) calculated. The Cronbach's alpha for the entire survey instrument yielded 0.844, indicating a high level of internal consistency. The Cronbach's alpha for each of the subscales was very good. This implies that the items measure a single concept with reasonably high inter-correlations. The standard rule of thumb is that reliability coefficients (alpha) should be at least or greater than approximately .70 to conclude that the scale is reliable for effective instruments (Wallen & Fraenkel, 2001). Results of the reliability test for each of the subscales (compound components) are shown as follows:

Table 4

Reliability Test for PSCAQ Subscales

Individual Items and Scales	Factor Loadings
Identity Consciousness and Home Nostalgia (Cronbach's alpha= 0.752)	
I miss my home country's food a lot.	0.639
I feel that I am able to relate well (interact) with American students in this country.	0.603
Talking to my family on the phone will always make me feel better.	0.536

I feel very unhappy (sad) easily when my ways of life are not accepted.	0.570
I feel like talking to my family back home everyday	0.514
I often feel that I have lost the ways of life of my family and other things we like in the family.	0.512
I am able to do well here what I used to do in my home country	0.458
I don't feel like going to the counselor's office for help even when I have problems.	0.460
I don't feel like myself in this country	0.458
I worry a lot about my family back home.	0.454
I have problems with American's way of life because of the way I was brought up in my family.	0.410

Psychological Disorientation and Cultural Inflexibility(Cronbach's alpha=0.789)

I do not feel safe in this country because of whom I am.	0.646
My people may think that I am mad or crazy if they see me going into the counselor's office for help.	0.610
I feel always unhappy with the American Culture (way of life).	0.596
I do not feel okay here in college because people here have ways of life different from mine.	0.598
I have problems with American's way of life because of the way I was brought up in my family.	0.527
This college does not have enough things that help students here as we have in my home country.	0.475

I don't trust American people for social interactions and lasting friendship.	0.547
What I have seen in my home country makes me not like to interact with teachers here.	0.465
I don't always feel safe simply because I am away from home.	0.469
I find it hard to trust other people's ways of life that are different from my own people's ways of life.	0.492
Americans do not accept other people's ways of life.	0.414
I don't feel like going to the counselor's office for help even when I have problems.	0.416

Family Attachment and Academic Maladjustment (Cronbach's alpha= 0.767)

I do not always feel safe simply because I am away from my family.	0.628
I miss our way of dressing a lot too.	0.584
I miss my family's support a lot in so many ways.	0.610
Talking to my family on the phone will make me not feel being alone (lonely).	0.615
I feel like I am alone here.	0.519
I put more time in classroom work and studies than in other things else so as to keep doing well.	0.440
I like talking to my family first before I do anything important here.	0.491

I always work hard more in class to pass well in order to make my family happy because that is what my people do (or are known for).	0.416
Education and learning in class here are more difficult than the one in my country.	0.455
I feel that I am not doing very well in class works because of my English.	0.400
Talking to my family on the phone will always make me feel better.	0.489

In this factor analysis, clusters of survey items were congregated around constructs associated with foreign-born students' psycho-cultural maladjustment indicators and criterion (dependent) variables. Categories, created after preliminary factor analysis, were narrowed from eight to three. These three scales replaced the original eight components.

Descriptive Factor Labels

I created descriptive factor labels for reports and subsequent analyses. Factors were labeled based on the aspect of which foreign-born students' psycho-cultural maladjustment characteristic they measure with a certain degree of reliability. Factor components extracted from an extensive literature review were utilized in this process. Correlated factors were combined after factor analysis and are branded compound components. They include identity consciousness and home nostalgia; psychological disorientation and cultural inflexibility; family attachment and academic maladjustment. Though the individual responses to each statement (survey item) will be useful, this researcher utilized three factors or scales that are more valid measures of FBSs psycho-cultural adjustment challenges at CCs in the Northeastern US. This description comprised both a combined measure of the items and factors associated with each scale. The new emerging constructs were labeled Scale A, Scale B, and Scale C.

Data Collection: Main Study

All data collections and recruitments from foreign-born students commenced with the initial approval by the Seton Hall University IRB. Data collection for the main research study involved three community colleges contacted by telephone and e-mail. With formal e-mail letters, I identified myself as principle researcher, provided the purpose for contact, the title of the dissertation and its purpose. I then requested permission to conduct research on the potential post-migration psycho-cultural adjustment challenges of FBSs at CCs. Community college representatives were assured that all responses from FBSs would be kept confidential and the data would be published in aggregate form only. Colleges contacted agreed to permit me to send packages of survey questionnaires to their CCs for this study. Parcels included a formal letter of solicitation and informed consent forms to FBSs, the 44 item survey questionnaire and large-size self-addressed return envelope.

Data collection was accomplished in two phases. The first phase involved the use of the survey instrument while the second phase involved the use of focus-group discussion protocol. I contacted the administrative departments and the Institutional Review Boards of the three participating CCs in the Northeastern United States to solicit approval for research.

First Phase

A copy of the letter of solicitation describing the purpose of the survey was e-mailed to all foreign-born students at the three community colleges. A package containing 1,250 copies of the survey instruments with a brief letter describing the study and statement of the Institutional Review Board's (IRB) approval to the representatives at the participating CCs. Copies of survey questionnaires were distributed to FBSs, who were available in various classes and willing to participate in the survey during class hours, by selected FBSs coordinators who are themselves FBSs. All participants were asked to fill out the questionnaires in class and return same to the designated FBSs' coordinators for the researcher. The whole survey data-collection exercise at the three participating CCs continued from December 8, 2011 until June 24, 2012.

Participants were asked to rate statements on a 5-point Likert scale (where 1= strongly disagree and 5=strongly agree). I provided the measures as the researcher-developed of the self-report questionnaire containing 36 items based on literature reviews related to psychological, cultural and psycho-cultural adjustment challenges of foreign-born students and migrants. The responses were computed for each subscale of adjustment. A high score, on related items, indicates that the respondent has potential post-migration psycho-cultural adjustment challenges and therefore may need help to improve while a low score implies that the respondent seems to be facing little or no challenges in that area of his or her life and may not need help to improve in that area.

Out of the survey instruments that were sent out for a target population of 1,650 foreign-born students, due to unanticipated restrictions, a total of 850 survey questionnaires were actually distributed to those FBSs who were available at selected community colleges. Follow-up survey e-mails were also sent out by two obliging CCs after two weeks to improve as well as maximize response rate. Out of the total 850 FBSs who received questionnaires, 441 respondents returned completed questionnaires. Responses with missing values for any of the items on the survey instrument were not included in the analyses. Fifteen surveys returned uncompleted were discarded, while 34 responses with missing values were excluded, leaving 382 complete and usable survey responses for the final sample, yielding a response rate of approximately 45%.

Response rates.

Out of the seven community colleges originally contacted, three agreed to allow their foreign-born students to be surveyed with one CC imposing some restrictions on this researcher. Surveys were delivered to the three participating CCs. Four hundred and forty-one students out of a total target population of 1,650 FBSs (approximately 27% return rate) completed survey. Responses with missing values on any of the items of the scales were not included in the final analysis. Those with missing values numbered 34 and accounted for approximately 8% of the responses. This process left me with 382 valid cases and usable data. According to Gay and Airasian (2003), a response of 60% or lower may lead to some questions about the generalizability of a study's results. The response rate for the present study is much lower than Gay and Airasian's threshold. Therefore, the results of this survey, though very enlightening, may not be generalized, not only because of the response rate, among other statistical reasons, but also because random sampling was not generated (Creswell, 2003; Krathwohl, 2004; Gay & Airasian, 2003). To protect the students' identity, FBSs were not required to write their names any place on the survey instrument.

Non participants

Brief consideration ought to be given to foreign-born students who chose not to participate in the study since non-participants, even a negligible number, could shape study results to a certain degree. Reasons abound why some FBSs may have chosen not to participate in this study. The first reason is language and linguistic deficiency. It is possible that those students who are not proficient in the English language may have found it uncomfortable to participate. Some FBSs may have felt reluctant to participate because research focused on a phenomenon that seems a bit probing, cognizant of cross-cultural elements that are profoundly idiosyncratic. In this case, some may have been suspicious of the researcher's motives and unwilling to put their view on the record (Hughes, 2004). Suffice it to mention that the target age bracket for this study is 18 years old and above. This means that all FBSs below 18 were excluded in this study. Another possible reason for reduced FBSs' participation may have been mere apprehension despite assurances that the anonymity of participants and confidentiality of responses would be preserved.

Second Phase

In a bid to gain access to and simultaneously recruit foreign-born student participants for the subsequent focus group session, flyers were posted on bulletin boards, and distributed at the community college centers, school libraries, and other local libraries during the survey data collection phase. Letters of interest and informed consent forms were also sent out by e-mail to three participating community colleges for their foreign-born students with my contact information attached just as it was on the fliers. I received some phone-calls and e-mail replies over the course of about two weeks. From about nineteen FBSs from the two CCs in New Jersey that signified interest either by e-mail, or phone call, nine were selected based on their proficiency in both spoken and written English. I also selected participants (FBSs) of mixed genders, from different countries, continents, academic programs, and age brackets. These selections were made from among those FBSs who responded to posters and flyers by either phone calls or e-mails. In making this selection, I hypothesized that such participants will enhance the issues from various perspectives and would make data more grounded and complete. One foreign-born student who called in at the last minute was added to the group, making their number ten. An e-mail message transmitted to the would-be participants and meeting was organized at a common venue in a free public school conference room in New Jersey. I requested that would-be participants provide written responses to the group discussion guide questions prior to meeting. A focus group session was conducted on June 27, 2012 with ten participants.

Ten foreign-born students submitted their written answers to guide questions and participated in a focus-group session. Key information from these written responses provided supplementary qualitative data. With the signed informed consent from international student participants I was able to initiate and facilitate the focus-group discussions that commenced at 3 o'clock in the afternoon and lasted for about one hour and twenty-five minutes. Prior to the focus-group session I briefly described the purpose of the study and introduced each participant without identifying them by name. The discussion then ensued regarding those factors considered significant to implicate post-migration psycho-cultural adjustment challenges of FBSs at the selected community colleges.

The focus-group discussion was open but directed by the guide questions that also provided structure to the discussions during which I was able to elicit detailed information and comments from the respondents (Rubin & Babbie, 2001). The 23 guide questions were compressed to nine questions for want of time. Related questions were combined in the process. Therefore, the focus group session entailed posing nine major questions to the participants with their responses tape-recorded and I subsequently transcribed them. The transcriptions were read several times with irrelevant materials deleted. The findings from the written responses as well as the transcribed information from the focus group session were abridged, coded, and analyzed to assist in the interpretation of the explanatory design participant selection model study. A little tangible compensation was given to each participant after the focus group session for volunteering to help a student researcher.

What is interesting is that many of the participants' stories were, to some extent, similar and each apparently corroborated the other. At some point, it seemed as though I was not learning anything new. No new categories emerged that could not fit easily and logically into an already existing category. At this juncture it was determined that a logical saturation point had been reached in this qualitative research.

Human Subjects' Protection

To ensure human subjects' protection, the Institutional Review Board at Seton Hall University (IRB) reviewed and approved all procedures prior to subsequent commitment to data collection. Provisions were made as well as precautions taken to ensure that the privacy, anonymity, and confidentiality of the institution and that of individual participants in the study were protected (Creswell, 2003; Krathwohl, 2004). The following steps were taken to preserve privacy, anonymity and confidentiality: foreign-born student volunteers were not required to record their names, social security numbers (if applicable), phone numbers, e-mail addresses, or even student identification numbers on the survey-response questionnaires. Personal identifiers of similar nature were not required for the focus-group session, either. In summary, I refrained from highly detailed descriptions of the participants and their community colleges of affiliation. Data and information from the survey exercise and focus group session were stored electronically on the USB memory key and I should retain these for at least three years in my secure private apartment. Only I had or have access to the completed survey data and focus session responses. The information obtained from the survey was reported only as group data for completing the dissertation. Each community college's designated personnel assisted me only in sending out e-mail messages to FBSs as well as helped to select FBSs who served as coordinators for in-class survey data collection. Recruitment of subjects for the focus-group discussions was done by distribution of flyers at selected CCs. Flyers were distributed to available FBSs as well as posted on the three CCs' bulletin boards by me and in some cases with the assistance of designated foreign-born student coordinators.

Description of Data Analysis

Data analysis comprised the examination of FBSs' answers to survey items and responses to focus group discussion questions and discussions. Data were analyzed using these categories: survey analysis and responses to focus-group discussion analysis.

Quantitative Analysis

Descriptive statistics

Frequencies and percentages for respondents' (FBSs') answers were calculated. In addition to a frequency table for gender-related responses, other continent, year in college and age-related variables were analyzed using descriptive statistics.

Inferential statistics

Analysis of variance (ANOVA) model was used to examine foreign-born students' gender, age, and continent of origin association with their post-migration psycho-cultural adjustment challenges. These tests examined the variations among different variables of male and female psycho-cultural adjustment challenges at community colleges in the Northeastern United States.

Survey Questionnaire Data Analysis

Table 5 summarizes the three research questions, the survey items that provided the data on those questions, and the data analysis done to answer those research questions. Frequency of responses and percentage mean was used to measure psycho-cultural adjustment challenges among the respondents.

Table 5

The Research Question and Subsidiary Questions' Analyses Approach

Research Question	Survey Items	Data Analysis
1. To what extent and in what ways do FBSs enrolled in CCs in the US face post-migration *psycho-cultural* adjustment challenges?	*5,7,9,11,12,32,31,36, 37,8,14, 33,15,34,24,10,22,21, 2,6,1,19, 20,16,23,25,4,29,26,2 8, 27, and 30*	• Descriptive Statistics • Descriptive Statistics • Inferential Statistics: ANOVA
2. To what extent and in what ways do post-migration psycho-cultural adjustment challenges differ among groups of FBSs (such as by gender, age, year in college, continents of origin, marital status and family presence) enrolled in CCs in the US?	*5,7,9,11,12,32,31,36,3 7,8,14,33,1,5,34, 24,10,22,21,2,6,19,16, 2,3,25,4,29,26,28, 27 and 30.*	• Descriptive Statistics
3. To what extent and in what ways are post-migration	*34,35,36,37,38,39,40, 41,42,43,44*	

psycho-cultural adjustment challenges related to the outcomes (such as Social Inter-action and Academic/Career Engagement) among FBSs enrolled in CCs in the US?

Qualitative Analysis

Inductive analysis

The three research questions were further answered using seven-step inductive analysis of the focus group discussion and discursive responses to their post-migration psycho-cultural adjustment challenges in a new environment at community colleges in the Northeastern United States. The data for this analysis was taken from the foreign-born students' responses to the 23 open-ended questions contained in the focus group discussion-guide questions. Inductive and interpretative analysis was performed on both the open ended oral and written responses to the discursive questions. Hatch (2002) defines inductive data analysis as "searching for patterns of meaning in available data so that general statements about phenomenon under investigation can be made" (p.161), while Thomas (2003) describes interpretive analysis as providing meaning that goes beyond the mere description of the data. Therefore, inductive and interpretive analysis in this study helped me as the researcher to give meaning to quantitative statistics, put pieces together in constructing explanations, and expand on findings from the inferential statistics for a better data interpretation.

For this study, foreign-born students' oral and written responses to focus group discussion questions were also analyzed in unison for common beliefs, thoughts, feelings, experiences, and opinions that FBSs expressed on their post-migration psycho-cultural adjustment challenges in a new culture and environment. Additional emergent themes were sought in those responses. Descriptions of emergent themes from responses have helped to support quantitative data analysis as well as elaborate on the data findings from a qualitative strand.

Focus Group Data Analysis

Transcribed and abridged information gathered from the focus group session coupled with complementary written responses from participants were immediately analyzed and coded. Codification of data into categories was done by refining and distilling participants' responses. I clarified the meaning of each category with distinctions created between categories and determination made regarding the most important categories needed for study. Data were analyzed using a seven-step approach and a constant comparative method whereby line, sentence and paragraph segments of the transcribed discussions and written responses were reviewed to decide what codes fit the concepts suggested by the data with the following, words, context, internal consistency, frequency and extensiveness, intensity of comments, specificity of responses and big ideas, put into consideration (Krueger, 1994; Krueger & Casey, 2000; Strauss & Corbin, 1998). Analysis transforms data into meaningful patterns and categories (Patton, 2002). The focus group data were used to further explain the survey data in the analysis. Similarities, differences and general patterns in each category were identified and the data arranged into a continuum of specific response patterns.

In summary, data were analyzed and reduced by means of thematic codes and process. Themes gradually emerged as a result of the combined process of becoming familiar with the data, making logical connections with the interview and research questions that link primary literature review. After conducting the initial analysis, member-checking was employed in collaboration with some of the participants in a follow-up contact to ensure that the thoughts and beliefs of the participants as reflected in the responses were properly represented (Creswell & Miller, 2002). I was able to locate all the ten participants who took part in the focus group session through one of the key participants. They all accepted the offer for transcription review. Copies were e-mailed to them and they returned responses confirming that transcription was properly done and was representative of their discussions.

Data Review

Data obtained from the focus group session were reviewed using specific research and interview questions as guidelines. Tapes from focus group session were initially transcribed verbatim, in order to capture the exact words, phrases, and inflections voiced by the participants, but later abridged. An abridged transcript, which consists of only 16 pages, is a condensed version of the focus group discussions with irrelevant and redundant dialogue removed. I independently identified six common themes across the responses to interview questions. These were later combined into three compound components to suit the 3 quantitative constructs in this present study.

To enable me to identify respondents without revealing their identities, unique identifiers such as female or male respondent 1, 2, 3, 4, and so forth were assigned to each participant in the focus group discussion. The transcripts were reviewed and intently examined tapes for emerging themes and patterns that relate to factors typifying post-migration psycho-cultural adjustment challenges among foreign-born students at community colleges.

Upon completion of the meeting, the focus group created a list of factors that they agreed upon that potentially constitute foreign-born students' post-migration psycho-cultural adjustment challenges. The list of the factors that appeared in the list of the focus group is shown in Table 4.

Data Coding

Coding is essentially the process of assigning the responses into categories or domains (Patton, 2002). For this research, the terms categorizing and coding were used synonymously. In order to simplify this process, I used the same basic format for coding guide as found below. The coding guide utilizes two formats for the coding design. Therefore, data coding is organized in two phases.

The first phase consists of broad categories, using three-factor domains influencing potential post-migration psycho-cultural adjustment of foreign-born students. These three components (identity consciousness and home nostalgia; psychological disorientation and cultural inflexibility; family attachment and academic maladjustment) were used as headings of the categories.

Table 6

Coding Guide Phase One (Using Abbreviated Heading Only)

CODE	DOMAIN (CATEGORY)
ICHN	Identity Consciousness & Home Nostalgia
PDCI	Psychological Disorientation & Cultural Inflexibility
FAAM	Family Attachment & Academic Maladjustment

In the second phase of the coding guide precise categories related to factors influencing FBSs post-migration psycho-cultural status were created. These categories enabled me to analyze data and further categorize the focus group responses in accordance with the psycho-cultural constructs to which they are most closely associated. Emerging themes, their frequencies and patterns were identified, enabling the compilation of a matrix of identifiable variables. The headings of the categories were abbreviated so as to appear meaningful and recognizable to the researcher for easy analysis as they appear in the next table:

Table 7

Coding Guide Phase Two (Using Abbreviated Heading Only)

CODE	SPECIFIC FACTORS INFLUENCING *PSYCHO-CULTURAL* ADJUSTMENT	FACTOR DOMAIN
ICHN	<ul><li>A strong 'inner feeling' of pride about one's culture and people</li><li>A certain feeling of *"uprootedness"* from one's former ways of life</li><li>Missing Home, Culture, unique social life, style of dress and food</li></ul>	Identity Consciousness & Home Nostalgia
PDCI	<ul><li>Difficulty accepting the entire American lifestyle</li><li>Belief that Americans have a different world view</li><li>Inability to easily adjust to Americans' stressful rush over life in general</li><li>A certain feeling like an 'outsider'</li><li>Some noticeable difference between Individualism and Collectivism; Conservatism and Liberalism in lifestyles</li><li>An inward feeling about some lack of respect for adults.</li><li>Little or no interest in going for counseling</li></ul>	Psychological Disorientation & Cultural Inflexibility
FAAM	<ul><li>Missing family so much enough because of closeness and intrinsic family values</li><li>Nuclear Family members have shared similarities</li><li>Family connection and attachment offers a sense of security</li><li>More rigorous and rigid academic system with strict school discipline down home</li><li>More active participatory nature of class engagement in the US</li><li>Belief in a more comprehensive and elaborate type of education in home country with a certain lack of depths</li><li>Different education standard surprises and flexibility of academic program choice</li></ul>	Family Attachment & Academic Maladjustment

Organizing Data

Focus group responses (data) were organized using summary interview guide questions. The previously abridged transcription of audio-taped responses facilitated this process. This approach was useful during the interpretation of the data because the emphasis on responses for which substantial agreement existed across various participants could be highlighted. Each individual interview guide question was listed along with its attendant probes on separate sheets of paper using a word processing program. Ample spaces were left beneath each question for subsequent responses from individual participants. Each participant's response, using unique identifiers, was listed beneath the question to which it corresponds.

Categorizing Data (Responses)

In this section, focus group responses (data) were categorized using the phase one coding guide. Identifying emerging themes and patterns was the ultimate goal of the focus group discussions. Categorizing factors from emerging themes and patterns enabled me to expose factors that influence post-migration psycho-cultural adjustment challenges of foreign-born students at community colleges. Three existing compound-factor components that influence post-migration psycho-cultural adjustment of FBSs were utilized to code responses from the focus group discussions.

I utilized a tape-based approach for data analysis that uses abridged transcripts of the relevant and useful portions of the focus group discussion as a basis for analysis (Krueger & Casey, 2000). The abridged transcript was supplemented with complementary written responses to the guide questions from focus-group participants. Since only one researcher was involved in this data analysis, using copies of transcripts and writing directly onto them with codes was the format employed.

Coding Focus Group Responses

Before drawing conclusions about data, I coded the focus group responses using the phase two portion of the coding guide (Table 7). Each response is linked to a specific factor influencing psycho-cultural adjustment (FIPCA) listed under the domain for which it was coded. These factors are directly associated with post-migration psycho-cultural adjustment challenges of foreign-born students at community colleges in the Northeastern US. I marked the linked responses using the code created for that specific FIPCA.

Interpreting Data

I made an explicit link between the focus group data and research objectives and subsequently identified patterns among the participants' responses, themes, and patterns that confirmed or contested the idea of potential post-migration psycho-cultural adjustment challenges of foreign-born students at community colleges in the Northeastern United States. Views, opinions, and responses that were unusual and distinctive among FBSs in relation to the factors influencing their post-migration psycho-cultural adjustment challenges at CCs were identified.

Chapter Summary

Much attention was given to the eight main sections of this chapter. The first section dealt with the mixed method approach used for this research design. The second dealt with the method used to incorporate pilot test factor and reliability analyses results. The third described the population and the fourth the sample of the research participants. The fifth section focused on the instruments utilized in this project. Data collection procedure and protocols for the main study were presented in the sixth section. The seventh section dealt with the human subjects' protection precautions. The eighth strand describes the researcher's data analysis procedures. In the next chapter I will display the analyses, results, and findings of this study.

CHAPTER IV
Analysis and Presentation of Findings

Introduction

This chapter presents analyses and findings garnered from conducting this study. The purpose of this study was used to examine post-migration psycho-cultural adjustment challenges of foreign-born students enrolled in community colleges in the Northeastern US. A mixed method (quantitative and qualitative) design was utilized in which qualitative data, derived from a focus group session, were used to shed light on the larger study (quantitative). Therefore, data were analyzed both quantitatively and qualitatively.

Research Questions

Three research questions that guided the research are as follows:

1. To what extent and in what ways do FBSs enrolled in CCs in the US face post-migration psycho-cultural adjustment challenges?

2. To what extent and in what ways do post-migration psycho-cultural adjustment challenges differ among groups of FBSs (such as gender, age, year in college, continent of origin, marital status and family presence) enrolled in CCs in the US?

3. To what extent and in what ways are post-migration *psycho-cultural* adjustment challenges related to the outcomes (Social Interaction and Academic/Career Engagement) of FBSs' adjustment at CCs in the US?

Dependent variables are broken down into three subscales. These subscales were derived after a factor analysis. The three resulting subscales were lettered A-C. The subscales are:
1. identity consciousness and home nostalgia.
2. psychological disorientation and cultural inflexibility.
3. family attachment and academic maladjustment. The independent and categorical variables in this study are: gender, age, marital status, country of origin, and year in college and family Presence in the US. The subscales were created to address the above research questions and subsidiary questions.

Organization of Chapter Contents

Data analysis is presented in five sections: (a) demographic profile of subjects (b) analyses of the research questions (c) linking potential post-migration psycho-cultural adjustment variables to foreign-born students' demographic data and (d) analysis of FBSs' adjustment outcomes. Section A presents the demographic profile of FBSs in the survey sample. Sections B addresses the three research questions based on FBSs' responses to the items on the scales and contains data relevant to items 1-36. Section C establishes link between psycho-cultural adjustment factors and the demographic characteristics. Section D addresses subsidiary question 3 in relation to demographic data and analyses relevant to FBSs' adjustment outcomes. This single section (d) also contains data and analysis relevant to items 40-44 as they impact the subscale items.

Tables associated with data are incorporated throughout the text and repetitive texts and semantics are used, as much as possible, to maintain uniformity and consistency of the data analyzed.

Demographic Profile of FBSs in the Survey Sample

Table 8 presents a demographic profile of FBSs included in this survey research study. Variables in the Table comprise: Age, gender, year in college and regions as well as continents of origin.

Table 8

Abridged Demographic Profile

Description (Characteristics)	Frequency	Percent
Gender		
Male	120	31%
Female	262	69%
Age		
18-25	190	50%
26-35	115	30%
36-45	48	12%
46-55	20	5%
56-65	3	1%
Over 65	6	2%
Marital Status		
Married	128	34%
Single	233	61%
Divorced	21	5%
Year in College		
Year one	211	55%
Year two	97	26%
Year two and over	74	19%
Continent		
Asia	81	21%
Latin America	172	45%
Europe	85	22%
Africa	17	5%
Middle East	14	4%
North America	13	3%
Family in the US?		
Yes	264	69%
No	118	31%
Total FBSs	382	100%

Sample Demographics (N= 382)

Twenty-one percent (21%) or 81 of international student respondents in this sample were from Asia; 45% (172) from Latin America; 22% (85) from Europe; 5% (17) from Africa; 4% (14) from the Middle East and 3% (13) from North America. With respect to gender, 69% (262) of the sample were female while male respondents were 31% (120). Total student participants ranged in age from 18 to 65 years and over. More of the students were in the 18-25 year old age range as compared to those in the 56-65 year-old range. As evident in the table, 34% (128) were married; 61% (233) of the students were single while 5% (21) were divorced. Fifty five percent (211) of FBSs were in their first year of studies; 26% (97) in their second year, while 19% (74) have completed their second year. 69% (264) of the respondents have family in the US while 31% (118) do not.

Analysis of Research Questions

Research Question 1: *To what extent and in what ways do FBSs enrolled in CCs in the US face post-migration psycho-cultural adjustment challenges?*

The first research question aimed to discover variables that demonstrate to what extent and in what ways foreign-born students face psycho-cultural adjustment challenges at community colleges. To best address this question, responses to survey items associated with psycho-cultural variables as well as suggested themes from the focus group discussions were sequentially analyzed. Survey items selected to address this question are distributed across subscales A, B and C as shown in Tables 9, 10, and 11.

Subscale A: Identity Consciousness and Home Nostalgia

This subscale A accounted for 17.1 percent of the variance. A total of eleven items were loaded onto this first subscale, labeled subscale A. This construct whose items were labeled identity consciousness and home nostalgia subscale, includes items that address research questions 1, 2, and 3. It captures six items of the ten items that dealt with foreign-born students' identity consciousness and the remaining five items that addressed home nostalgia. Those items are used to elicit respondents' thoughts, feelings, and experiences at the community colleges, based on their psycho-cultural adjustment challenges. A Likert-type subscale was used to measure each item with the following subscale category descriptions: 1= Strongly Disagree; 2= Disagree; 3= Neutral; 4= Agree; 5= Strongly Agree. The mean scores on the Likert-type subscale ranged from 2.17 to 3.58, and the standard deviation, from 1.007 to 1.226 (see Table 9). The subscale has a total mean of 2.7291 and the standard deviation of 0.62104. All survey items are presented in table form in Appendix A.

Table 9

SUBSCALE A: Identity Consciousness and Home Nostalgia

Survey Items *Variable	Mean	Std. D	SD	D	N	A	SA	Cum-Ag	Cum-Dis
Miss my home country's food a lot.	3.05	1.226	8.1%	32.5%	21.2%	22.5%	15.7%	38.2%	40.6%
Feel able to relate well (interact) with American students in this country.	2.83	1.120	12.0 %	31.7%	22.3%	29.3%	4.7%	32.7%	34.0%
Talking to my family on the phone will always make me feel better.	3.58	1.131	4.5%	16.2%	18.6%	38.7%	22.0%	60.7%	20.7%
Feel very unhappy (sad) easily when my ways of life are not accepted.	2.45	1.051	17.3%	44.0%	22.0%	13.9%	2.9%	16.8%	61.3%
Feel like talking to my family back home everyday	2.74	1.060	10.2%	37.4%	25.7%	22.0%	4.7%	27.7%	47.6%
Often feel having lost my family's ways of life and other things we like in the family.	2.52	1.039	14.1%	43.2%	22.3%	17.0%	3.4%	20.4%	57.3%
Able to do well here what I	3.49	1.098	15.4%	30.4%	19.4%	28.0%	6.8%	34.8%	45.8%

Item	Mean	SD							
used to do in my home country									
Don't feel like going to the counselor's office even when I have problems.	2.28	1.064	25.9%	38.7%	17.8%	15.2%	2.4%	17.6%	64.6%
Don't feel like myself in this country	2.17	1.007	25.9%	46.3%	14.4%	11.3%	2.1%	13.4%	72.2%
Worry a lot about my family back home.	2.86	1.198	13.6%	30.1%	22.3%	22.5%	8.9%	31.4%	43.7%
Have problems with American's ways of life because of the way I was brought up.	2.11	0.957	27.2%	46.9%	15.4%	8.9%	1.6%	10.5%	74.1%

*Items collectively designate criterion (dependent) variables under consideration.

On subscale A, eight of eleven items have means below 3.0. Data analyses for the eleven listed items, with a sample size of three hundred and eighty two (N=382), indicated that FBSs' respondents strongly disagreed or disagreed to all the six items related to both identity consciousness and to four of the five items related to home nostalgia on subscale A. This analysis assumes that foreign-born students' responses to each item on the subscale most likely reflect their thoughts, feelings, and opinions about themselves in relationship with the phenomenon under study. Also, putting this finding within the context of identity consciousness (IC) and home nostalgia (HN) sub-constructs would suggest that FBSs at the participating community colleges do not have potentials for psycho-cultural adjustment challenges that are strongly based on the distribution of their responses to items linked to IC and HN on subscale A.

Responses to the six items assessing FBSs' identity consciousness which comprise, "I don't feel like myself in this country," "not feeling like visiting the counselor even when I have problems," "I feel very unhappy easily when my ways of life are not accepted," "I often feel having lost the ways of life of my family and other things we like in the family," "I like to relate only with people from my own area or home country because I feel comfortable doing that," and "I have problems with Americans' way of life because of the way I was brought up in my family," are shown in Table 9.

In terms of how identity consciousness (IC) as a potential factor influencing their psycho-cultural adjustment at community colleges, most foreign-born students indicated by their responses to related items that IC was not necessarily an influential factor. Fifty-nine and four-tenths of a percent (59.4%) of FBSs disagreed or strongly disagreed to the items on the subscale A associated with IC; 20.2% agreed or strongly agreed to the items on the subscale A associated with IC, while 20.4% maintained neutrality in response to the items associated with IC on subscale A.

Responses to the five other items assessing foreign-born students' home nostalgia which comprise: "I am able to do well here what I used to do in home country", "I miss my country's home food a lot," "I worry a lot about my family back home," "I feel like talking to my family back home every day," and "Talking to my family on the phone will always make me feel better," are also shown in Table 9.

In terms of how home nostalgia (HN) as a potential factor influencing their psycho-cultural adjustment at CCs, most FBSs indicated, by their responses to related items that HN was not an influential factor. 39.6% of FBSs disagreed or strongly disagreed to the items on the subscale associated with HN. 38.6% agreed or strongly agreed to the items on the subscale associated with HN, while 21.8% maintained neutrality in response to the items associated with HN on subscale A. Strikingly, when one examines the variables in relationship to the other and the distribution of IS responses to items linked to the HN subscale, it is noteworthy that the sample group of FBSs is almost equally divided in response to the items on this sub-construct.

A summary of the above descriptive statistics indicates that the sample group reflected in this subscale responded more to ten of the eleven items on subscale A (identity consciousness and home nostalgia) with some degree of disagreement. However, it can be found in Table 9 that while a large number of foreign-born students responded to most items in the negative (with disagreement), evidence abound that in some cases a relatively significant number of FBSs responded to items in the affirmative (with agreement). We can observe from the above exhibit that FBSs disagreed to this statement: "I miss my country's home food a lot" almost in the proportion at which they agreed to same. 40.6% (155) disagreed while 38.2% (146) agreed to the same. Interestingly, FBSs also disagreed and agreed to two more items in slightly large proportions, respectively. For instance, 45.8% (175) of FBSs disagreed to the following statement: "I am able to do well here what I used to do in home country," while 34.8% (133) agreed to the same. In a similar vein, 41.6% of FBSs disagreed to the following statement: "I like to relate only with people from my own area or home country because I feel comfortable doing that," while 32.7% agreed to the same. Surprisingly, 60.7% of FBSs item who, expectedly, agreed that "Talking to their families on the phone would always make them feel better" produced a mean average response of 3.05 on subscale A. Even though the mean value of responses to both the suggestion of being able to do well here what one used to do in one's own home country and the idea of missing one's home country's food a lot are greater than the researcher's set midpoint of 3.0, the real value differences may not be determined with certainty in an ordinal subscale. However, it is noteworthy that because a higher-number of international student respondents (modes = 175, 155 & 232) disagreed to both the suggestion of being able to do well here what one used to do in one's own home country and the idea of missing one's home country's food a lot while agreeing to the suggestion that talking to family on the phone will always make one feel better respectively, it can, therefore, be assumed, with some degree of justification, that FBSs are more likely to disagree to the idea of being able to do well here in the US what they used to do in their own home country and the idea of missing their home country's food a lot on subscale A.

The number of foreign-born students who gave neutral responses to items on the subscale with a mean total of 20.9% (79) responses is also worthy of consideration. Therefore, the number of respondents that checked neutral will not be excluded from the final analysis. Based on the mean scores in the above distribution, we can see that majority of IS respondents, with the mean total response of 49.5% (189), indicated some degree of disagreement to items on the subscale while 29.6% (114) agreed or strongly agreed to items on the subscale. Given the pattern of responses and the substantial number (114 out of 382) that agreed to items on the subscale, overall, FBSs are most likely to disagree or strongly disagree to the items on subscale A. This statistical data, therefore, does not suggest any need for critical attention, or improvement on FBSs' psycho-cultural adjustment challenges associated with both identity consciousness and home nostalgia.

Subscale B: Psychological Disorientation and Cultural Inflexibility

This subscale B accounted for 9.6 percent of the variance. A total of twelve items were loaded onto this second subscale, labeled subscale B. This construct whose items were labeled psychological disorientation and cultural inflexibility subscale, includes items that address research questions 1, 2, and 3. It captures five items of the twelve items that dealt with FBSs' psychological disorientation and the remaining eight items that addressed cultural inflexibility. Those items are used to elicit respondents' thoughts, feelings, and experiences at CCs in the Northeastern US, based on their psycho-cultural adjustment challenges. Please note that survey item 18 did not load onto the subscale B and was omitted from analysis. A Likert-type subscale was used to measure each item with the following subscale category descriptions: 1= Strongly Disagree; 2= Disagree; 3= Neutral; 4= Agree; 5= Strongly Agree. The mean scores on the Likert-type subscale ranged from 2.11 to 2.80, and the standard deviation, from 0.898 to 1.200 (see Table 10). The subscale has a total mean of 2.3346 and the standard deviation of 0.56542. All survey items are presented in table form in Appendix A.

Table 10

SUBSCALE B: Psychological Disorientation and Cultural Inflexibility

Survey Items *Variable	Mean	Std. D	SD	D	N	A	SA	Cum -Ag	Cum - Dis
Not feeling safe in this country because of whom I am.	2.17	.952	24.9%	45.5%	18.8%	9.4%	1.3%	10.7%	70.4%
My people thinking me mad/crazy going into the counselor's office help.	2.22	.898	19.1%	51.3%	19.1%	9.4%	1.0%	10.4%	70.4%
Feeling always unhappy with the American culture.	2.41	1.020	27.2%	46.9%	15.4%	8.9%	1.6%	10.5%	74.1%
Not feeling okay in college because of ways of life different from mine.	2.11	.957	16.2%	38.5%	25.9%	16.8%	2.6%	19.4%	54.7%
Have problems with American way of life because of the way I was raised.	2.34	1.032	19.6%	44.8%	21.7%	9.7%	4.2%	13.9%	64.4%
CC lack things that help students as we have in my home country.	2.71	1.194	16.0%	33.8%	21.7%	20.4%	8.1%	28.5%	49.8%

Don't trust American people for social life and lasting friendship.	2.32	1.003	19.9%	44.2%	22.8%	9.9%	3.1%	13.0%	64.1%
Experiences back home discourages me from interacting with teachers here.	2.18	.976	25.7%	44.5%	17.8%	10.7%	1.3%	12.0%	70.2%
Don't always feel safe simply because I am away from home.	2.73	1.015	8.1%	33.0%	21.2%	23.0%	15.7%	38.2%	41.1%
Find it hard trusting ways of life different from my own people's.	2.26	.942	20.2%	45.8%	23.3%	8.9%	1.8%	10.7%	66.0%
Americans do not accept other people's ways of life.	2.28	1.200	25.9%	38.7%	17.8%	15.2%	2.4%	17.6%	64.6%
Don't feel like going for counseling even when I have problems.									

*Individual items collectively designate criterion (dependent) variables under consideration

In subscale B, all the twelve items have means below 3.0. Data analyses for the twelve listed items, with a sample size of three hundred and eighty two (N=382), indicated that IS respondents strongly disagreed or disagreed to the items related to both psychological disorientation and cultural inflexibility on subscale B. This analysis assumes that foreign-born students' responses to each item on the subscale most likely reflect their thoughts, feelings, and opinions about themselves in relationship with the phenomenon under study. Putting this finding within the context of psychological disorientation (PD) and cultural inflexibility (CI) sub-constructs would suggest that FBSs at the participating CCs do not have potentials for psycho-cultural adjustment challenges based on the distribution of their responses to items linked to the above two factors (PD and CI) on subscale B.

Responses to the five items assessing foreign-born students' psychological disorientation which comprise, "Not feeling safe in the country because of who I am," "Not feeling like visiting the counselor even when I have problems," "People thinking me crazy going for counseling," "I don't always feel safe away from home," and "What I have seen in my own country makes me not like to interact with teachers here," are shown in Table 10.

In terms of how psychological disorientation (PD) as a potential factor influencing their psycho-cultural adjustment at the CC, most foreign-born students indicated by their responses to related items that PD was not an influential factor. Sixty-six and nine-tenths percent (66.9%) of FBSs disagreed or strongly disagreed to the items on the subscale associated with PD and 13.8% agreed or strongly agreed to the items on the subscale associated with PD, while 19.3% maintained neutrality in response to items associated with PD on subscale B.

Responses to the seven items assessing foreign-born students' cultural inflexibility which comprise, "Feeling always unhappy with the American culture," "Not feeling okay in college," "Have problems with

Americans' ways of life," "Finding it hard to trust other people's ways of life different from my own people's ways of life," "Not trust Americans for social interactions and lasting friendship," "College does not have enough resources," and "Americans do not accept other people's ways of life" are also shown in Table 10.

In terms of how cultural inflexibility (CI) as a potential factor influencing their psycho-cultural adjustment at the community college, most foreign-born students indicated, by their responses to related items that CI was not an influential factor. Sixty percent (60%) of FBSs disagreed or strongly disagreed to the items on the subscale associated with CI; 18.8% agreed or strongly agreed to the items on the subscale associated with CI, while 21.2 % maintained neutrality in response to the items associated with CI on subscale B. Interestingly, when one examines the variables in relationship to the other, it is noteworthy that the sample group of FBSs is almost equally divided in response to the statement that "finding it hard to trust other people's ways of life different from my own people's ways of life." In this particular case, 40.6% (155) of FBSs disagreed while 38.20% (146) agreed.

A summary of the above descriptive statistics indicates that the sample group reflected in this subscale, responded overwhelmingly to all of the items on subscale B in disagreement. However, it can be found in Table 10 that while a large number of foreign-born students responded to most of the items in the negative, evidence abounds that in some cases a relatively significant number of FBSs responded to items in the affirmative. The number of FBSs that gave neutral responses to each of the items with a mean total of 20.4% (78) responses is also worthy of consideration. Therefore, respondents that remained neutral would not be excluded from the final analysis. Based on the mean scores in the above distribution, we can see that the vast majority of international student respondents, with the mean total response of 61.2% (233), indicated some degree of disagreement to items on the subscale, while 18.4 % (71) agreed or strongly agreed to items on the subscale. Overall, given the pattern of responses, FBSs are most likely to disagree or strongly disagree to the items on subscale B. This statistical data, therefore, does not suggest any need for critical attention, or improvement on FBSs' psycho-cultural adjustment challenges associated with both psychological disorientation and cultural inflexibility.

Subscale C: Family Attachment and Academic Maladjustment

This subscale accounted for 7.4 percent of the variance. A total of ten items were loaded onto this third subscale, labeled subscale C. This construct whose items were labeled family attachment and academic maladjustment subscale, includes items that address Research Questions 1, 2, 3. It captures seven items out of eleven items that dealt with FBSs' family attachment and the remaining four items that addressed academic maladjustment. Those items are used to elicit respondents' thoughts, feelings, and experiences at CCs in the Northeastern US, based on their psycho-cultural adjustment challenges. A Likert-type subscale was used to measure each item with the following subscale category descriptions: 1= Strongly Disagree; 2= Disagree; 3= Neutral; 4= Agree; 5= Strongly Agree. The mean scores on the Likert-type subscale ranged from 2.29 to 3.66, and the standard deviation, from 1.052 to 1.353 (see Table 11). Subscale C has a total Mean of 3.2474 and the Standard Deviation of 0.64664. See Appendix A for all survey items.

Table 11

SUBSCALE C: Family Attachment and Academic Maladjustment.

Survey Items *Variable	Mean	Std. D	SD	D	N	A	SA	Cum-Ag	Cum-Dis
Don't always feel safe simply because I am away from my family.	3.09	1.114	5.8%	30.6%	21.7%	32.2%	9.7%	41.9%	36.4%
Miss our way of dressing a lot too	3.19	1.353	13.6%	21.5%	18.1%	25.7%	21.2%	46.9%	35.1%
Miss family's support a lot in so many ways.	3.21	1.162	5.2%	27.7%	22.8%	28.8%	15.4%	44.2%	39.9%
Talking to family on the phone will make me not feel being alone.	3.66	1.054	4.7%	9.7%	20.4%	44.8%	20.4%	65.2%	14.4%
Feel like I am alone here.	2.29	1.083	13.4%	23.8%	19.4%	27.7%	15.7%	43.4%	37.2%
Put more time in classroom work and studies than in other things else so as to keep doing well.	3.31	1.103	6.3%	18.6%	25.7%	36.9%	12.6%	49.5%	24.9%
Like talking to my family first before doing anything	3.42	1.149	5.5%	18.6%	22.5%	34.8%	18.6%	53.4%	24.1%

important here.									
Work hard more in class to pass well in order to make my family happy because that is what my people do.	3.48	1.052	4.7%	14.4%	22.8%	44.0%	14.1%	58.1%	19.1%
Education and learning in class here are more difficult than the one in my country.	2.90	1.249	13.4%	30.9%	20.4%	23.0%	12.3%	35.3%	44.3%
Feel not doing very well in class works because of my English.	3.10	1.103	7.6%	23.6%	27.0%	34.8%	7.1%	41.9%	31.2%
Talking to my family on the phone will always make feel better.	3.58	1.131	4.5%	16.2%	18.6%	38.7%	22.0%	60.7%	20.7%

*Items collectively designate criterion (dependent) variables under consideration.

In subscale C, nine of the eleven items have means above 3.0. Data analyses for the eleven listed items, with a sample size of three hundred and eighty two (N=382), indicated that international student respondents agreed or strongly agreed to the items related to both family attachment and academic maladjustment on subscale C. This analysis also assumes that foreign-born students' responses to each item suggestion on the subscale most likely reflect their thoughts, feelings, and opinions about themselves in relationship with the phenomenon under study. Putting this finding within the context of family attachment (FA) and academic maladjustment (AM) sub-constructs would suggest that FBSs at CCs do have potentials for psycho-cultural adjustment challenges based on the distribution of their responses to items linked to FA and AM on subscale C.

Responses to the seven items assessing foreign-born students' family attachment which comprise the following: "I feel like I am alone here," "I miss our way of dressing a lot too," "I do not always feel safe simply because I am away from home," "I miss my family's support a lot in so many ways," "Talking to my family on the phone will make me not feel being alone," "I like talking to my family first before I do anything important here." and "Talking to my family on the phone will always make feel better," are depicted in Table 11.

In terms of how family attachment (FA) as a potential factor influencing their psycho-cultural adjustment at community colleges, most foreign-born students indicated by their responses to related items that FA was to some relatively great extent an influential factor. Forty-nine percent (49.0%) of FBSs agreed or strongly agreed to the items on the subscale associated with FA; 31.2% disagreed or strongly disagreed to the items on the subscale associated with FA, while 19.8% maintained neutrality in response to items associated with FA on subscale C.

Responses to the four items assessing FBSs' academic maladjustment which comprise the following: "Education and learning in class here are more difficult than the own in my country", "I always work hard more to pass well in order to make my family happy because that is what my people are known for", "I put more time in classroom work and studies than in other things else so as to keep doing well " and "I feel that I am not doing very well in class works because of my English" are also shown in Table 11.

In terms of how academic maladjustment (AM) as a potential factor influence their psycho-cultural adjustment at community colleges, most foreign-born students indicated, by their responses to related items that AM was to some relatively great extent an influential factor. 46.2% of FBSs agreed or strongly agreed to the items on the subscale associated with AM. 29.9% disagreed or strongly disagreed to items on the subscale associated with AM, while 23.9 % maintained neutrality in response to the items associated with AM on subscale C.

A summary of the above descriptive statistics indicates that the sample group of foreign-born students reflected in this subscale overwhelmingly responded to all of the items on subscale C with agreement. However, it can be found in Table 11 that while a large number of FBSs responded to most of the items in the affirmative (agreement), evidence abound that in some cases a relatively significant number of FBSs responded to the items in the negative (disagreement). When one examines the item variability in relationship to the subscale, it is noteworthy that 35.3% (135) of FBSs agreed to the idea that "education and learning in class here are more difficult than the own in my country" while 44.3% (169) disagreed to the same. Agreeable responses from FBSs to the suggestions of not always feeling safe simply because one is away from home and the feeling of not doing very well in class works because of one's English are equal in proportion. 41.9% (160) of FBSs agreed to both items in equal proportions. On the other hand, 36.4% (139) of FBSs disagreed to the ideas of not always feeling safe simply because I am away from home while 31.2% (119) of FBSs disagreed to the feeling of not doing very well in class works because of one's English.

The number of FBSs that gave neutral responses to each of the items with a mean total of 22.1% (84) responses is also worthy of consideration. Therefore, respondents that remained neutral would not be excluded from the final analysis. Based on the mean scores in the above distribution, we can see that the vast majority of IS respondents, with the mean total response of 48% (183), indicated some considerable degree of agreement to items on the subscale, while 29.9% (115) disagreed or strongly disagreed to items on the subscale. Overall, given the pattern of responses, FBSs are most likely to agree or strongly agree to the items on subscale C. This statistical data, therefore, suggest a certain level of need for critical attention, as well as improvement on FBSs' psycho-cultural adjustment challenges associated with both family attachment and academic maladjustment.

Research Question 2: *To what extent in what ways do post-migration psycho-cultural adjustment challenges differ among groups of FBSs (such as gender, age, year in college, continent of origin, marital status and family presence) enrolled in CCs in the US?*

This subsidiary research question sought to identify differences in demographic variables of gender, age, continents and subcontinents in relationship to foreign-born students' adjustment challenges. To address this research question, trends were described and mean scores compared across groups of FBSs based on gender, age, and on their major continents and subcontinents of origin. This question is addressed by all the 34 survey items distributed in Tables 9, 10, and 11 while linking demographic variables and Psycho-cultural adjustment challenges. FBSs' post migration psycho-cultural adjustment challenges may be influenced by some demographic subscales. The purpose of this section is to examine the influence of FBSs' demographic data on their potential post-migration psycho-cultural adjustment challenges at CCs.

Analyses of Variance (ANOVA)

Analyses of variance (ANOVA) models were computed to evaluate differences between group scores on the three psycho-cultural adjustment subscales. Trends were described as well as mean scores compared across groups of FBSs based on gender, age, marital status, continents of origin, year in college and family presence variables. The impacts of these demographic variables on FBSs' psycho-cultural adjustment challenges were calculated. Tukey's Honestly Significant Differences (HSD) post hoc analysis was selected to determine mean differences between pairs of groups when significance was found. Significance value was set at the .05 level.

Table 12

Effects of Gender on FBSs' Psycho-cultural Adjustment

	Gender	Sum of Squares	df	Mean Square	F	Sig
Subscale A	Between Groups	1.365	1	1.365	1.367	.243
	Within Groups	379.635	380	.999		
	Total	381.000	381			
Subscale B	Between Groups	3.761	1	3.761	3.789	.052
	Within Groups	377.239	380	.993		
	Total	381.000	381			
Subscale C	Between Groups	.088	1	.088	.088	.767
	Within Groups	380.912	380	1.002		
	Total	381.000	381			

One-way ANOVA test of Between-Subjects Effects in Table 12 revealed that there are no statistically significant differences between male and female foreign-born students, in terms of their psycho-cultural adjustment challenges at CCs based of the three-subscale output, $P>.05$. Subscale A: $F(1,380) =1.376$, $p=.243$; subscale B: $F(1,380) =3.789$, $p=.052$ and subscale C: $F(1,380) =0.088$, $p=.767$. Therefore, when placing the level of significance of .05 against these computations in each of the three subscales, the null hypothesis (no differences between groups), if applicable; stated or assumed, is accepted. This implies that there is no statistically significant difference in the outcome between male and female FBSs' psycho-cultural adjustment. Therefore, the data and results in this chapter mandate the acceptance of any existing or assumed null hypotheses. The means and standard deviations of the paired groups according to FBSs' gender were tabulated as follows: Subscale A (Male= -0.09, SD= 0.92; Female: M= 0.04, SD= 1.03); subscale B (Male: M= 0.15, SD= 1.03; Female: M= -0.07, SD= 0.98) and subscale C (Male: M= -0.02, SD= 1.03; Female: M= 0.01, SD= 0.99).

The above finding is incongruous with earlier studies on foreign-born students' psychological and sociocultural adjustment challenges which suggest that female FBSs' experience more psychological disorientation strain, during the period of adjustment, than their male counterparts. In like manner, other studies that examined FBSs showed that female students had higher emotional, physiological, and behavioral reactions to adjustment stressors and are also more likely to feel homesick and lonely than were male students (Misra, Crist, & Burant, 2003; Rajapaksa & Dundes, 2003). Consistent with the findings of this particular study on gender influence Sumer, Poyrazli, & Grahame (2008) found no association between gender and FBSs' depression and anxiety levels as potential components of psychological disorientation.

Table 13

Effects of FBSs' Age on their Psycho-cultural Adjustment

	Age	Sum of Squares	df	Mean Square	F	Sig
Subscale A	Between Groups	40.202	5	8.040	8.871	.000
	Within Groups	340.798	376	.906		
	Total	381.000	381			
Subscale B	Between Groups	4.260	5	.852	.850	.515
	Within Groups	376.740	376	1.002		
	Total	381.000	381			
Subscale C	Between Groups	15.919	5	3.184	3.279	.007
	Within Groups	365.081	376	.971		
	Total	381.000	381			

One-way Analysis of variance (ANOVA) output indicates statistically significant differences in *age* between groups on subscales A (identity consciousness and home nostalgia) and c (family attachment and academic maladjustment), in terms of the psycho-cultural adjustment challenges of foreign-born students at community colleges. This means that there are statistically significant differences ($p < 0.05$) in age impact on FBSs' psycho-cultural adjustment at CCs based on different age ranges of 18-25; 26-35; 36-45; 46-55; 56-65 and over 65. Subscale A: $F(5,376) = 8.871$, $p = .000$ and subscale C: $F(5,376) = 3.279$, $p = .007$. Therefore, when placing the level of significance of .05 against these computations in each of the two subscales (A&C), the null hypothesis (no differences between groups), if applicable; stated or implied, is rejected.

Tukey's HSD post hoc test was utilized to evaluate the pairwise mean differences between groups on subscale A (identity consciousness and home nostalgia). Pairwise comparisons of the means indicated that the mean score of foreign-born student respondents within the age group of 18-25 (M= 0.13, SD= 0.98) significantly differs from those within the age groups of 46-55 (M= -0.90, SD=0.70); 56-65 (M = -1.47, SD = 0.17) and over 65 (M= -1.15, SD = 0.54). However, it was not higher than those within the age groups of 26-35(M= 0.15, SD= 0.95) and 36-45 (M= -0.28, SD= 0.99).

The mean score of foreign-born student respondents within the age group of 26-35(M= 0.15, SD= 0.95); significantly differs from those within the age groups of 46-55 (M= -0.90, SD=0.70); 56-65 (M = -1.47, SD = 0.17) and over 65 (M= -1.15, SD = 0.54). However, it did not significantly differ from those within the age groups of 18-25 (M= 0.13, SD= -0.98) and 36-45 (M= -0.28, SD= 0.99).

Tukey's HSD pairwise comparisons of the means on subscale C (family attachment and academic maladjustment), indicated that the mean score of foreign-born student respondents within the age groups of 18-25 (M= 0.07, SD= 1.04); 26-35 (M= 0.04 SD=1.01) and 36-45 (M= 0.07, SD= 0.79) significantly differs from those within the age group of 46-55 (M= -0.76, SD=0.72). However, they did not significantly differ from those within the age groups of 56-65 (M = -0.78, SD = 0.91) and over 65 (M= -0.47, SD = 0.70).

The mean scores of foreign-born student respondents within the age group of 26-35(M= 0.04 SD=1.01) was found to significantly differ from those within the age groups of 46-55 (M= -0.76, SD=0.72). However, it did not significantly differ from those within the age groups of 18-25 (M= 0.07, SD= 1.04); 36-45 (M= 0.07, SD= 0.79) 56-65 (M = -1.47, SD = 0.17) and over 65 (M= -1.15, SD = 0.54).

Taken together, these results suggest that *Age* does have an effect on the identity consciousness and home nostalgia as well as on the family attachment and academic maladjustment aspects of foreign-born students' psycho-cultural adjustment challenges at community colleges. Specifically, this study suggests that FBSs within younger age groups of 18-25 (M= 0.13, SD= 0.98); 26-35 (M= 0.15, SD= 0.95) and 36-45 (M= -0.28, SD= 0.99) reported having problems with identity consciousness and home nostalgia more than older age groups of 46-55 (M= -0.76, SD=0.72); 56-65 (M = -1.47, SD = 0.17) and over 65 (M= -1.15, SD = 0.54). Likewise, FBSs within younger age groups of 18-25 (M= 0.13, SD= 0.98); 26-35 (M= 0.15, SD= 0.95) and 36-45 (M= -0.28, SD= 0.99) reported that they have problems with family attachment and academic maladjustment more than FBSs within the older age groups of 46-55 (M= -0.76, SD=0.72); 56-65 (M = -1.47, SD = 0.17) and over 65 (M= -1.15, SD = 0.54).

Consistent with this finding, Sumer et al., (2008) found that age subscales contributed uniquely to the variance in anxiety as a component of psychological disorientation. However, contrary to this finding, they further suggested that older foreign-born students were more likely to report higher levels of anxiety since they may be more traditional, more resistance to change, and have more trouble accepting the host culture's norms and values and therefore, experience higher levels of anxiety during their adjustment period. On the other hand, Tomich, McWhirter, & Darcy (2003) opined that the younger the FBSs, the faster and easier the adjustment process on a foreign soil.

Table 14

Effects of Marital Status on FBSs' Psycho-cultural Adjustment

	Marital Status	Sum of Squares	df	Mean Square	F	Sig
Subscale A	Between Groups	4.368	2	2.184	2.198	.112
	Within Groups	376.632	379	.994		
	Total	381.000	381			
Subscale B	Between Groups	9.510	2	4.755	4.851	.008
	Within Groups	371.490	379	.980		
	Total	381.000	381			
Subscale C	Between Groups	1.597	2	.799	.798	.451
	Within Groups	379.403	379	1.001		
	Total	381.000	381			

One-way ANOVA test on subscale B (psychological disorientation and cultural inflexibility) revealed that foreign-born students' marital status was statistically significant ($p < .05$) in their psycho-cultural adjustment challenges at the community colleges. Subscale B: $F(2,379) = 4.851$, $p = .008$. This means that there are statistically significant differences in marital status impact on the psycho-cultural adjustment outcome between groups of FBSs who are single, married, or divorced. Therefore, when placing the level of significance of .05 against these computations on the affected subscale (B); the null hypothesis (no differences between groups) if applicable, expressed or implied is rejected. This means that there are statistically significant differences in marital status impact between groups in this study.

Tukey's HSD post hoc comparisons of paired marital status groups on subscale B (psychological disorientation and cultural inflexibility), indicated that the mean score of the group of married IS respondents (*M* = -0.22, *SD* = 1.04) significantly differs from those that are single (*M*= 0.11, *SD* = 0.96) vice versa. However, the mean score of the group of divorced (*M* = 0.17, *SD*= 0.96) IS respondents did not significantly differ from the married (*M* = -0.22, *SD* = 1.04) and single (*M*= 0.11, *SD* = 0.96) international student respondents in this subscale.

Taken together, these results suggest that marital status does have an effect on the psychological disorientation and cultural inflexibility aspect of foreign-born students' psycho-cultural adjustment challenges at CCs. Specifically, this study suggests that FBSs who are divorced and single reported that they experienced psychological disorientation challenges as well as have potentials towards cultural inflexibility more than those FBSs who are married.

Table 15

Effects of FBSs' Continents and Regions on their Psycho-cultural Adjustment

	Continents and Regions	Sum of Squares	df	Mean Square	F	Sig
Subscale A	Between Groups	6.508	5	1.302	1.307	.260
	Within Groups	374.492	376	.996		
	Total	381.000	381			
Subscale B	Between Groups	8.404	5	1.681	1.696	.135
	Within Groups	373.096	376	.991		
	Total	381.000	381			
Subscale C	Between Groups	35.432	5	7.086	7.710	.000
	Within Groups	345.568	376	.919		
	Total	381.000	381			

One-way analysis of variance (ANOVA) model between group in Table 15 shows a statistically significant effect of continent of origin on foreign-born students' *psycho-cultural* adjustment in relation to subscale C (family attachment and academic maladjustment; $p<.05$). $F(5,376) =7.710$, $p=.000$. This implies that there are statistically significant differences in the continent of origin impact on the psycho-cultural adjustment outcome between groups of FBSs from Asia, Latin America, Europe, Africa, Middle East, or North America. Therefore, when placing the level of significance of .05 against these computations on subscale C, the null hypothesis (no differences between groups), if applicable; stated or implied, is rejected.

Tukey's HSD post hoc comparisons of paired groups of FBSs from different continents and subcontinents on subscale C (family attachment and academic maladjustment; $p<.05$, indicated that the mean score of the group of IS respondents from Europe (M = -0.30, SD = 0.98) differs significantly from those from Africa (M = 0.43, SD = 0.77), Middle East (M = 0.51, SD =0.96) and North America (M=1.20, SD =1.15). However, it did not differ significantly from those from Latin America (M = -0.08, SD = 0.85) and Asia (M = 0.11, SD = 1.14).

The mean score of the group of foreign-born student respondents from Latin America (M = -0.08, SD =0.85), differs significantly from those from North America (M=1.20, SD =1.15). However, it did not differ significantly from other groups of FBSs from the Middle East (M = 0.51, SD =0.96), Europe (M = -0.30, SD = 0.98), Africa (M = 0.43, SD = 0.77) and Asia (M = 0.11, SD = 1.14).

The mean score of the group of respondents from Asia (M = 0.11, SD = 1.14), differs significantly from those from North America (M=1.20,

SD =1.15). However, it did not differ significantly from other groups of FBSs from the Middle East (M = 0.51, SD =0.96), Europe (M = -0.30, SD = 0.98), Africa (M = 0.43, SD = 0.77) and Latin America (M = -0.08, SD = 0.85).

Taken together, these results suggest that continent of origin does have an effect on the family attachment and academic maladjustment aspect of foreign-born students' psycho-cultural adjustment challenges at community colleges. Specifically, given the mean scores, this test indicates that FBSs from North America, the Middle East, Africa, and Asia reported having more family attachment and academic maladjustment challenges than FBSs from Europe and Latin America.

Table 16

Effects of FBSs' Year in College on their Psycho-cultural Adjustment

	Years in College	Sum of Squares	Df	Mean Square	F	Sig
Subscale A	Between Groups	4.091	2	2.045	2.057	.129
	Within Groups	376.909	379	.994		
	Total	381.000	381			
Subscale B	Between Groups	6.112	2	3.056	3.090	.047
	Within Groups	374.888	379	.989		
	Total	381.000	381			
Subscale C	Between Groups	1.334	2	.667	.666	.514
	Within Groups	379.666	379	1.002		
	Total	381.000	381			

One-way ANOVA of Between-Subjects test effects in subscale B above (psychological disorientation and cultural inflexibility) indicates that year in college is statistically significant ($p<0.05$). Subscale B: $F(2,379) =3.090$, $p=.047$. This means that there are statistically significant differences in the year in college impact on the psycho-cultural adjustment outcome between groups of foreign-born students in year one, year two, or above year two at the community colleges.

Tukey's HSD post hoc comparisons of paired year in college groups of foreign-born student respondents in subscale B (psychological disorientation and cultural inflexibility); indicated that the mean scores of the groups of FBS respondents in year one (M = 0.05, SD = 1.00); year two (M= -0.06, SD =1.07) as well as year 2 and beyond (M = -0.07, SD = 0.91) did not significantly differ from each other in this subscale. However, from the look of the mean scores and the standard deviations, FBS respondents in year one were more likely to have responded more to the items on subscale B (psychological disorientation and cultural inflexibility) than the rest of the paired groups of those year two and beyond year two.

Taken together, these results suggest that year in college does have an effect on the psychological disorientation and cultural inflexibility aspect of foreign-born students' psycho-cultural adjustment challenges at community colleges. Specifically, given the mean scores, this study suggests that FBSs in year one are more likely to be impacted by psychological disorientation as well as have issues with cultural inflexibility problems than those in year two and above year two at CCs.

Table 17

Effects of FBSs' Family Presence in US on their Psycho-cultural Adjustment

	Yes and No	Sum of Squares	Df	Mean Square	F	Sig
Subscale A	Between Groups	10.064	1	10.064	10.310	.001
	Within Groups	370.936	380	.976		
	Total	381.000	381			
Subscale B	Between Groups	.637	1	.637	.636	.426
	Within Groups	380.363	380	1.001		
	Total	381.000	381			
Subscale C	Between Groups	.010	1	.010	.010	.919
	Within Groups	380.990	380	1.003		
	Total	381.000	381			

One-way ANOVA test between groups shows that family presence in the US is statistically significant ($p<0.05$) in the identity consciousness and home nostalgia aspect of foreign-born students' psycho-cultural adjustment challenges as depicted in subscale A. Subscale A: $F(1, 380) = 10.310$, $p = .001$. This means that there are statistically significant differences in the family presence impact on the psycho-cultural adjustment outcome between groups of FBSs who have families here in the US and those who do not. When placing the level of significance of .05 against these computations in each question, the null hypothesis, if applicable stated or implied, (no differences between groups) is rejected.

The means and standard deviations of the paired groups according to foreign-born students' family presence are as follows: Subscale A (Yes: $M=$ -0.11, $SD=$ 0.94; No: $M=$ 0.24, $SD=$1.08); subscale B (Yes: $M=$ 0.03, $SD=$1.02; No: $M=$-0.06, $SD=$ 0.96) and subscale C (Yes: $M=$ -0.0034, $SD=$ 1.05; No: $M=$ 0.0077, $SD=$ 0.89). This descriptive statistic indicates that FBSs (the no group) who reported that they did not have their families present in the US reported having more identity consciousness and home nostalgia issues than FBSs (the yes group) who indicated having their families present in the US.

Research Question 3: *To what extent and in what ways are post-migration psycho-cultural adjustment challenges related to the outcomes (such as Social Interaction and Academic/Career Engagement) among FBSs enrolled in CCs in the US?*

In an attempt to address this question, the frequency statistics of the foreign-born students' responses to survey items (outcome items) in Table 18 were calculated. Disaggregation and subsequent aggregation of FBSs' responses to associated outcome items determine the impact of their psycho-cultural adjustment challenges at the community colleges under study. This would enable the researcher determine to what extent and in what ways post-migration psycho-cultural adjustments variables correlate with, as well as impact FBSs' social interaction, retention and career engagement. This subsidiary question is primarily addressed by all the eight items on *Table 18*.

Table 18

Frequency Statistics for Outcome Variables (Survey Items 37-44)

Outcome Items (*Variable)	Yes	No	(DNK)*
Plan to continue your studies in this college?	41.9%	32.7%	25.4%
Plan to return home after your studies at this college?	52.4%	27.0%	20.6%
Feel like dropping out of the community college?	15.7%	63.1%	21.2%
Plan to enroll in a four-year college/university when you finish in this college?	26.2%	54.2%	19.6%
In general, satisfied with your life in this college?	68.3%	13.4%	18.3%
Select this CC given the opportunity to begin your study again?	75.6%	9.7%	14.7%
Select the US given the opportunity to begin your study again?	76.2%	9.7%	14.1%
Recommend the US to other students in your country who plan to study abroad?	81.6%	7.1%	11.3%

*(DNK) denotes Do not know or I Do not know

As illustrated in Table 18, responses to six of eight items in the affirmative (yes), indicate the level of impact psycho-cultural adjustment challenges have on foreign-born students' academic and career engagement. Respondents were asked the following questions: "Do you plan to continue your studies in this college?" Do you plan to return home after your studies at this college?" "In general, are you satisfied with your life in this college?" "Given the opportunity to begin your study again, would you select this community college as your place of study?" "Given the opportunity to begin your study again, would you select the US as your place of study?" "Would you recommend the US to other students in your home country who plan to study abroad?"

Foreign-born students were presented with three options: *Yes, No* and *Do not know* (DNK). In response to the question: *"Do you plan to continue your studies in this college?"* 41.9% (160) of FBSs found the idea of continuing their studies at their college appealing by indicating *yes*. 32.7% (125) found it less appealing by indicating *no*. A total of 25.4% (97) were on the borderline by indicating *do not know*. In response to the question *"Do you plan to return home after your studies at this college?"*, the top choice on *yes* was 52.4% (200), this significantly differs from what had been expected followed by 26% (103) who indicated *no* and 20.6% (79) for *Do not know*. Approximately sixteen percent (60) responded *yes* to the suggestion: *"feeling like dropping out of the CC?"* 63.1% (241) responded *no* while 21.2% (81) remained neutral by indicating *Do not know*. About twenty six percent (100) of FBSs responded yes to *"plans to enroll in a four-year college/university when you finish in this college?"* while a surprisingly large number of FBSs totaling 54.2% (207) noted that they would not enroll in a four-year college/university upon completion at the community college. The remaining respondents, totaling 19.6% (75) remained neutral by indicating do not know. These are represented in Bar charts. See figures 2 to 5 on the next page.

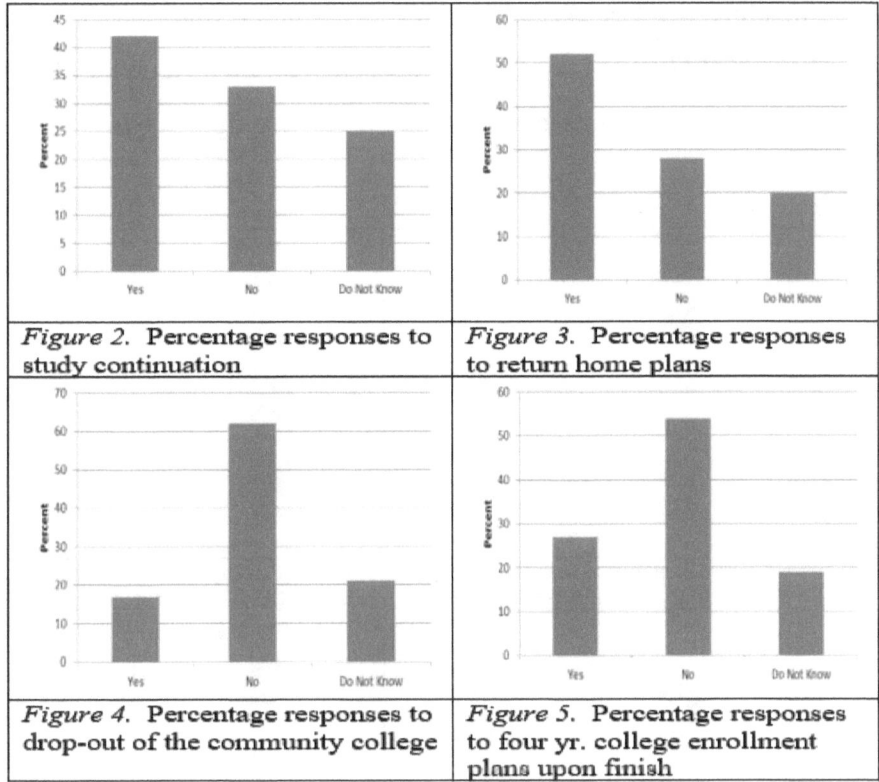

Figure 2. Percentage responses to study continuation

Figure 3. Percentage responses to return home plans

Figure 4. Percentage responses to drop-out of the community college

Figure 5. Percentage responses to four yr. college enrollment plans upon finish

Among foreign-born students who responded to the question which seeks to find out whether FBSs are satisfied with life in general at the CC, 68.3% (261) indicated yes, 13.4% (51) indicated no while the remaining 18.3% (70) checked do not know. On the question about selecting the CC as a place of study given another opportunity, 75.6% (289) indicated yes; 9.7% (37) responded no while 14.7% (56) indicated do not know. A higher number of respondents; 76.2% (291) indicated yes to the item which has to do with "wishing to select the US again as a place of study if given another opportunity to do so?"; 9.7% (37) indicated no to the same item while 14.1% (54) indicated do not know to the same item. 81.6% (312) of FBSs responded yes to the question which has to do with recommending the US to students in their country who wish to study abroad; 7.1% (27) responded no, while 11.3% (43) responded do not know. These are also represented in Bar charts. See figures 6 to 9.

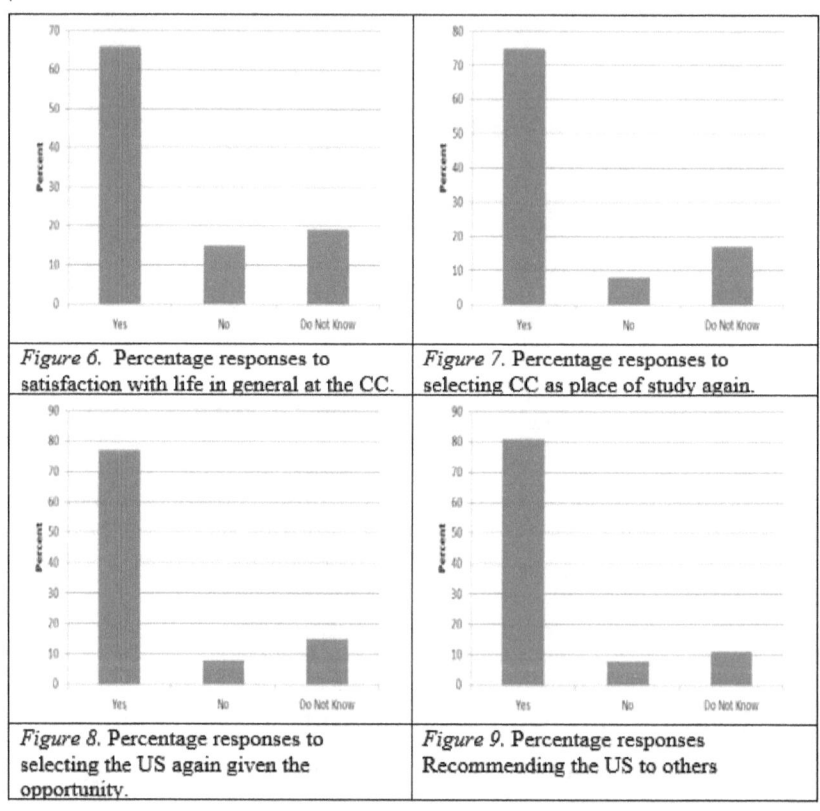

Figure 6. Percentage responses to satisfaction with life in general at the CC.	*Figure 7.* Percentage responses to selecting CC as place of study again.
Figure 8. Percentage responses to selecting the US again given the opportunity.	*Figure 9.* Percentage responses Recommending the US to others

Overall, indications of foreign-born students' desire for retention and career engagement in a foreign land are prevalent in the above distribution of FBSs' responses. This subsidiary research question was further addressed by all the items on *Table 19*.

Table 19

Complementary items Addressing Research Question 3 (FBSs' Adjustment Outcome Variables)

Survey Items *Variable	Mean	Std.D	SD	D	N	A	SA	Cum-Ag	Cum-Dis
Feel able to relate well (interact) with American students in this country.	2.83	1.120	12.0%	31.7%	22.3%	29.3%	4.7%	34.0%	43.7%
Feel comfortable relating only with people from my own area or home country.	2.85	1.122	12.3%	29.3%	25.7%	26.7%	6.0%	32.7%	41.6%
Experience back home discourages me from interacting with teachers here.	2.32	1.003	19.9%	44.2%	22.8%	9.9%	3.1%	13.0%	64.1%

Based on foreign-born students' responses to specific survey items selected to address subsidiary question 3; with the mean level of interest set at 3.0, Table 19 indicates that the total items had average mean scores of 2.67 making them less important for variable support. The mean score indicated that international student participants are relatively well-adjusted socially based on their responses to each of the complementary outcome items above. Surprisingly and unexpectedly, item variability shows that 43.7% (167) of foreign-born students at participating community colleges do not feel able to relate well (interact) with

American students in the US. Among those, 33.1% (130) indicated that they are able to relate well with Americans in the US while 22.3% (85) of international student participants remained neutral. However, 41.6% (159) disagreed to relating only with people from their own area or home country because they feel comfortable doing so. Additionally, 32.7% (125) responded in agreement while 25.7% (98) remained neutral.

Even though a relatively significant number of foreign-born students agreed to relating only with people from their own area or home country because they feel comfortable doing so the overall majority of FBSs' responses to related items suggests a remarkable level of improvement in FBSs' social adjustment (interaction) given their tendency to relate more with those from their own culture or country of origin. More than sixty-three percent (145) of FBSs disagreed with the suggestion that any experience in their own country keeps them from interacting well with teachers here. Furthermore, 12.1% (50) agreed that suggestion while 22.8% (87) remained neutral. That an overwhelming majority of FBSs disagreed with this suggestion signifies yet another level of improvement in social adjustment (faculty-student interaction). Also given the degree of neutral responses to these outcome items the number of foreign-born students' neutral responses may not be excluded from the final analysis.

Focus Group Session
Overview of focus group

A focus group session was conducted as a part of the research program that examines the psycho-cultural adjustment challenges of foreign-born students at community colleges in the Northeastern US. Focus group participants included 10 FBSs. Of this sample, 80% (8) were female while 20% (2) were male. Participants' ages ranged from 21 to 34 years.

Focus group data analyses

In-depth thematic analyses of the focus group data corroborated the result of the findings on the quantitative study. Besides, the relationship among the themes of this data pointed to the reconceptualization of the interaction among the psycho-cultural adjustment components. However, based on the focus group analysis, the overarching theme for the ten participants appeared to be the strong attachment FBSs feel toward their various families and homes thereby implicating family attachment and home nostalgia as the major sub-constructs in this study. Most participants discussed family attachment as significant reporting its strong influences on their psycho-cultural adjustment in college. Participants noted their families' influence on education, and other important decision makings. In general, all participants described family connection and contact as morally encouraging as well as emotionally and psychologically supportive.

Identity Consciousness and Home Nostalgia
(A) Identity consciousness

The data presented here contains foreign-born students' concise descriptions of both their self and group identities. It emphasizes participants' perception of themselves and their countries of origin including adjustment abilities based on their individual, societal and cultural strengths. This is based on their experience, thoughts and feelings about their own people's ways of life and the American people's ways of life. Overall, there was a clear indication of strong inner feelings of pride about their own cultures and peoples. A few participants' expressions of some feeling of uprootedness in the form of identity loss, missing home, culture, unique social life, clothing, hair style, style of dress and food are further illustrative of a certain level of identity consciousness and home nostalgia. These illustrations could easily be found in the following statements:

> "Well, as a Jamaican, I think there are many things.... that allow us to be who we are. In Jamaica, education is a part of the core of development. Parents believe that children must go to school. When children get education and they're mature, they look back and they're very grateful of the way we look at life. You know, we -- we're fighters for success. And so, because of that, when my culture says you're a goal getter, it's out there, go for it. Only the best is good enough and we are going to aspire for it." (North American female, age 34, 2nd year, married).

> "Well, my people in the Dominican Republic live their lives, and enjoy it despite adversity. We are happy people by nature. We face problems, but in a different approach. We do not always stress out in Dominican Republic. There's no need for that, if things can be so different." (South American female, age 31, 2nd year, married).

> "We have such a rich cultural background that the older generations of my parents, tend to see life in a more comprehensive way." (Asian female, age 29, 3rd year, single).

> "My people believe that, you know, you have to take care of your family, you have to work, you have to work hard....And not give

up. My mother, for example, even as an adult, kept going to school, and for example, when she was going to get a license and she kept trying and not gave up. Also, we have pride in our country. Even though we're not a big country, we still take pride in our history…. And absolutely we take pride in our flag and our country. Even though we are not the richest, you know, the worst side is what, you know, most people actually know about Haiti. But still Haitians know about, they know their history, and their pride; their Haitian pride." (North American male, age 28, 2nd year, single).

"My West Indies' rearing taught me different values." (South American female, age 21, 1st year, single).

"It is true that I miss our ice cream, kebabs', traveling to different tourist towns….but I still love our traditional music, our teahouses where they served us full meals, kebabs and rice grains. For instance, rice grains are very important to our people. By eating our own rice food, our people feel as if we are getting close to our maker. We also have different types of bread, our local vegetables…and our rice too." (Middle Eastern male, age 27, 3rd year, single).

"But it's totally different in my country because there, people care for you but here people think that they are perfect." (South American female, age 28, 2nd year, single).

In general, during the discussions, participants expressed a high level of appreciation for their home cultural values and identities. One could easily perceive a shared sense of community pride that connects a group of people in a given society. For instance, a female respondent from Asia alluded to her sense of pride in the following way:

"Whereas I feel like South East Asians are more lenient, and buoyant in dealing with their lives. For example, I noticed that lot of Americans only get married on a weekend. Whereas the Indian wedding lasts for five days, and it starts on Monday and ends on a Friday. And --- nobody really cares about going to work on Monday. You know? They just have the wedding for the entire week." (Asian female, age 27, 3rd year, single).

This female respondent gives us the impression that Indians attach a special meaning, importance and perspective to marriage. They perceive marriage as not just a ceremony or a celebration between two people, but as a special and communal expression of feelings among members of different families as well as a life-long commitment. In other words, the way people view certain aspects of their culture such as marriage, very much depends on the whether they were brought up and educated in the same vein. Male respondents from North America and the Middle East also made these enlightening remarks:

"Even though we're not a big country, we still take pride in our history.... And absolutely we take pride in our flag and our country." (North American male, age 28, 2nd year, single).

"It is true that I miss our ice cream, kebabs', traveling to different tourist towns....but I still love our traditional music, our teahouses where they served us full meals, kebabs and rice grains." (Middle Eastern male, age 27, 3rd year, single).

Attaching special meaning, importance, and perspective to things is also applicable to elements, products and materials in other people's culture. Take the case of food materials. Certain food items that are taken for granted in some places because its abundance might be the life blood of people in other cultures. Here in the US, it is possible that rice grains might have been taken for granted because of the assortment of its produce and ease of importation. Nevertheless, rice grains could also be regarded as something ravishingly exotic in other cultures. Aside from intangible (invisible) aspects of a people's culture, tangible (visible) aspects of culture could often connote rich cultural ideas for a group of people, with shared values and customs. Besides food materials, these might include things like articles of clothing, hairstyles, music, jewelry, sculptures and other cultural products. The focus group discussions revealed that someone from the Middle East might consider eating their own rice grains or eating our own rice food with some feelings of special connection with the divine. The male respondent from the Middle East, concerning their food materials, made the following remarks:

> "For instance, rice grains are very important to our people. By eating our own rice food, our people feel as if we are getting close to our maker. We also have different types of bread, our local vegetables…and our rice too." (Middle Eastern male, age 27, 3rd year, single).

People therefore behave according to their shared and internalized cultural values, attitudes, belief system, norms, philosophical assumptions, ideologies, customs, and principles.

(B) Home nostalgia

In response to whether they thought there was something they were missing at home, participants expressed feelings of home nostalgia with family contacts and home connections. Some participants reported difficulty in adjustment just because they missed home and things connected to home.

> "I miss home when it comes to way of dressing, eating, dancing, treating each other, culture, social behavior, driving, education system, religion issues, government, and so on. I miss our type of ice cream, kebabs', and traveling to different tourist towns." (Middle Eastern male, age 27, 3rd year, single).

> "I know I feel different at my home country. I love going home to visit and it is hard every time I leave to come back here." (European female, age 25, 2nd year, single).

> "It is comfortable to live here but sometimes I miss my family and my country's food. I mean I love it here but I prefer my country more (Asian female, age 29, 3rd year, single)."

> "When I left my country as an au pair I was very unhappy. I decided to go the England to try to find happiness in the UK before coming to the US – it didn't work, and that is why I am here today. I didn't feel it was a place for me anymore. I didn't actually know what my place was. All I knew I would not want to study in Europe

so, there must be something about this country. I'm not saying I am completely happy about everything here. I still think about home." (European female, age 25, 2nd year, single).

"After I left my country, I was feeling horrible. It was very difficult for me because I have never been so far from my country. I was homesick because I missed my family and friends a lot." (South American female, age 28, 3rd year, single).

"When I first came here…I felt sad and lonely. I felt like going back to Haiti, my country of birth." (North American male, age 28, 2nd year, single).

From the participants' responses I was able to conclude with conviction that there are to some extent, issues of identity consciousness and home nostalgia difficulties affecting foreign-born students' psycho-cultural adjustment at community colleges in the Northeastern US. Profound analyses of the participants' remarks would create a clear mental imagery that migration from one's own country, albeit for legitimate reasons, could trigger some sense of guilt generated by the stress of simply leaving one's own people. Some of these stresses are related to sudden separation from one's family, extended relations, friends, unique social life, style of dress and food. Interactive discussions with participants revealed that there is always an unrivalled feeling of uprootedness like that of someone; who is evacuated, experiences, coupled with an attendant feeling of isolation in a new culture and environment. Unfounded regrets that there was never enough time to prepare for migration also emerged. These feelings can come in the forms of worries about family members, special places, items, and facilities left behind at home, worries about the conditions of home and allied communities back home. In addition to other remarks related to home nostalgia, this is further exemplified in this type of innately strong nostalgic remarks:

> "I miss home when it comes to way of dressing, eating, dancing, treating each other, culture, social behavior, driving, education system, religion issues, government, and so on. I miss our type of ice cream, kebabs', and traveling to different tourist towns."
> (Middle Eastern male, age 27, 3rrd year, single).

Even though, circumstances of religious brutality, discrimination and persecution seem to have brought about this respondent's migration to the US, he completely appreciates and relishes his immigration status. However, he expresses some deep feelings of home nostalgia despite his much improved and, otherwise, enviable adjustment situation. Depending on individual migrant's circumstances and mission, these types of home nostalgic feelings can sometimes make it a bit challenging for a foreign-born student especially when it comes to getting around and adjusting smoothly in a new culture and environment. Such feelings could also become aggravated in a dramatically unfamiliar cultural milieu or in a status quo where two cultures are diametrically opposed to each other.

Psychological Disorientation and Cultural Inflexibility
(A) Psychological Disorientation

Of all the subscales identified as significant by participants, the issue of psychological disorientation did not emerge as critical in foreign-born students' psycho-cultural adjustment struggles. Discounting fundamental personality and temperamental characteristics, the majority of the participants noted that they often experienced feelings of loneliness, anxiety and near depression during the adjustment period. Going by the trajectory of the focus group discussions and from all indications there are various experiences and feelings that either presuppose or generate psychological disorientation. These include, language barrier, a feeling of helplessness, a feeling that no one cares, and a feeling of inadequacy as we shall further discover.

In response to the question: "Could you tell me the nature of some of the problems you have with American people's ways of life? Do you think that there is something you are missing at home? What are they?" discussants made the following excerpted revelations:

> "However, I've had my own setbacks as a student at this community college coming from Jamaica, West Indies. I believe, lots of problems, although this was a period of adjustment. There were times where I was lost and lonely and I had culture shock. And because of that I felt like no one truly understands or cares what I was going through, you know? Everyone's struggling for survival and it's harder for students who are not born in this country to really adjust to some of the changes. However, it depends on your mindset to some extent, because no matter how hard it was for me I decided within myself that my aim and objective was to become an overcomer. And it depends on the circumstances and the matter of a point whereby even though the coping skill was very hard I decided that no matter what the struggles are, those struggles I was having, I was an older student, so it was a matter of adaption with young students laughing at your accent and all different things. It was a matter of doing work and it becomes too wordy. And instead of the professor understanding my culture, is that it appears though I have to do a communication book because of the deep accent that I have from my country.

However, because of determination, I decided to just do the best I could and decided no matter what, I would succeed. So, when I look back on it I'm very happy." (North American female, age 34, 2nd year, married).

"Coming from the Dominican Republic, at first, when I first arrived here, was a little rough for me. Because of language barrier, I went through a lot of struggles. And it was kind of rough. The roughest spot for me was when I had to do homework, again, because of the lack of the language, the language barrier, limited me a lot from doing my homework on my own. My parents worked; my sisters worked, so I had no one to really help me. And then I have the teachers telling my co-students to not speak to me in Spanish, but in English. But that made me a stronger person in the ESL class." (South American female, age 31, 2nd year, married).

"I think I had a slightly opposite experience.... from the two previous speakers. But I have lived the system as well as experienced and live Indian culture, so that I can make a fair judgment. My mom was an educator, I had a primarily English speaking home, but I also learned my dominant mother tongue. But when I went to school, I went to school with primarily people who also went to India. I lived in a neighborhood where there are a lot of Indians. And so, I went to the ESOL classroom, which is when I got tested. They did an oral test on me. I was very shocked by me joining the…And so, I was put in ESOL classroom. And so, I was around people who were from the same area I was. And, therefore, I felt very comfortable in school. Because, I don't call myself American, I do believe I have a hyphenated identity. So, it's just, it -- I do, but I do feel like this is home. So, it's strange." (Asian female, age 27, 3rd year, single).

"For me, the transition at first was psychologically challenging because I came into this country not knowing the language, and the culture. However, the area I am living is mostly black. And so, it is different. It is a different experience for me definitely. And I graduated eventually from high school." (North American male, age 28, 2nd year, single).

"America has so many restrictions, laws and rules to follow. Back home was easier but I always had distractions that prevented me from doing school work. No., because I lived a completely different lifestyle back in my country compared to here. A lot of differences, but it's okay at the moment because we all have to make sacrifices to achieve our goals in life. Really there are a lot of differences between living here in America and living at home. It is very different. Each culture has its own components. In Rome, do what Romans do. It is good to be here because it helps you to be on your own, to be independent in a place where everybody is rushing to survive. It helps you to learn how to do things and manage your life. Back home parents, siblings and friends help and support you but no support here. Yes, I miss friends and family and the beautiful beaches." (South American female, age 21, 1st year, single).

"If it comes to the things that I miss from home that I don't have here it is definitely my family. I see them only once a year in the summer when I go home. I love to spend time with them. I love the polish food we cook together with my mom. I try to cook polish dishes here too, but somehow it is not the same. If it is not for the ingredients, then it is the company. Nothing feels better than having a meal with your family. I think if my family was able to come and visit me once a while, it would make a big difference." (European female, age 25, 2nd year, single).

"No, I don't feel like I am at home. There is still prejudice towards immigrants specially the ones that come here to professionally grow in life. Also, I don't feel like I am at home here because I have intrinsic family values that I hardly find on people born in this country. I believe everything is ok the way I feel because I understand there are differences of cultures and I am the one who should adapt to the different culture. I am not pretentious to believe I will become "one of them" but I also understand that this country is a melting pot. I don't think the right question is what can make me feel better. If I am not up to challenges I should never had left my country. USA is the way it is and I am the one who should adapt. The countries values and people's cultures are what make this country attractive to foreigners. I understand I have different cultures and the people from this country also have to understand my culture and values because I have met the entire pre requisites to come here. I really miss my natural language, culture, food, friends, and missed my family. I don't stop thinking about them. I also think this is my second home. I feel good here but of course this is not my country. If my family were here, I would feel completely at home." (South American female, age 28, 2nd year, single).

"No, I really don't care! I don't even know what the difference in culture between my home country and the American culture would be. All I know is that I'm beginning to feel at home here. I do my best every day to understand and appreciate the American culture, relate well with people here; I have no choice. I think that I am okay with every culture. I don't really miss so much but I still love our traditional music, our teahouses where they served us full meals, kebabs and rice grains. For instance, rice grains are very important to our people. By eating our own rice food, our people feel as if we are getting close to our maker. We also have different types of bread, our local vegetables…and our rice too I think I miss them somehow but that's okay." (Middle Eastern male, age 27, 3rd year, single).

"I feel that people here do not help each other and don't care to understand other people's culture. Sometimes, I try to explain to them why it is different….I feel bad because they don't understand our lives. Right now, I'm very good because, every day I improve my life by doing better in my English. Yes, I still miss my family, my friends and home food especially our common lunch at home. I miss our music and our way of dressing. I miss so much my family. I miss the love of how my grandmother cooked the food. I miss them a lot because I never was far away from them." (South American female, age 28, 3rd year, single).

The above illustrating quotations from the focus group participants reveal foreign-born students' stark awareness of some differences in culture, values, and lifestyle between their home countries and country of sojourn. It is a clear testimony that people from different places tend to think differently, perceive differently, feel differently, as well as act differently based on their assimilated cultural values. These reports from focus-group respondents show that FBSs inherited some values from their countries that fundamentally define them for who they are and have left some lasting configurations in their pattern of thinking, feeling, and presentation of the self. These are evident in the remarks from the first and second female respondents and more clearly evident in the response from the first female participant who believed that those values constituted a part of their core cultural (psycho-cultural) development.

Moreover, participants' remarks uncover a certain degree of difficulty adjusting to American lifestyles and values among foreign-born students in general, perhaps as a result of the accumulation and internalization of those deep cultural values. Such difficulties could be indications of potentials towards cultural inflexibility or identity consciousness that constitute major offshoots of the post migration psycho-cultural maladjustment factors under investigation in this study. Identity consciousness also emerged in some of the participants' recognition of differences in other major psycho-cultural orientations styled: individualism/universalism/achievement and collectivism/ particularism/ascription as well as conservatism and liberalism of lifestyles (Hofstede, 2000; Trompenaars & Hampden-Turner, 1997 & 1998). A further investigative probe into the meanings of these assertions would confirm that FBSs' perceive Americans (US nationals) as not only considering themselves but also acting as independent and important members of the society. These perceptions of Americans by FBSs may represent accurate observations of the hallmarks and characteristics of individualism/universalism/ achievement-oriented cultural values playing out both in social roles and in interpersonal relationships.

On liberalism and conservatism, participants believe that foreigners are very conservative as compared to Americans who are more liberal. This Asian female respondent believes that conservatism is relative to each generation as well as evolutionary:

> "My parents' generation of South Koreans, were very old fashioned, traditional and conservative….but the newer and younger (her own) generation are more modernized and westernized; meaning being more liberal." (Asian female, age 29, 3rd year, single).

She saw liberalism and conservation as different ways of thinking that are basically leveraged on certain values. Her perception of liberalism is also suggestive of one's freedom to follow what are obtainable in a modern society rather than adhere to one's traditional and hereditary values. The female respondent from South America believes that the United States' liberal values sprang from their constitutional rights to liberty and freedom of expression of their feelings that are not easily obtainable in her own country. Some participants perceived this freedom in everything as having been overstretched into passivity regarding some perceived lack of respect for adults in the host culture. They further signified that any attempts at a total imbibition of such models of freedom and liberty might introduce some level of misunderstanding and conflict in their family relationships as well as possibly fracture their core cultural developmental values which seldom exposed them to such levels of freedom and liberty. There seemed to have been a common agreement among FBSs over American peoples' rushing, workaholic, uptight and stressful lifestyle. This is also subjectively based on their own perception based on the aforementioned differences in cultural values and orientations.

In reaction to a specific question about going to mental health counseling which runs as follows: "Do you ever think about going for mental health counseling? What would you tell me now can make you not go for mental counseling? Give me examples of those reasons?" The following responses emerged from the foreign-born student participants' discussions:

> "I've never thought that I was in any serious need of going for mental health counseling because we are a strong people, we are independent people. We are always known for bouncing back and never give up. I might need counseling only for anything that affects a better life for me and my family. I think that I will seek counseling only when I'm no longer able to help myself and have no body around in my family to help me." (North American female, age 34, 2nd year, married).

> "I am not used to asking for help from people outside my family and so I will not feel comfortable going for counseling. Maybe it might help. I may think about doing that if I have any big problem that I can't solve with my family." (South American female, age 31, 2nd year, married).

> "You know both of my parents are from India. We don't really feel comfortable going for mental health counseling. Now, I'm

learning how to help myself here in America when I have problems. My people, I mean my family, and friends, will laugh in your face to hear that you are going for mental counseling. They will be looking at you as a 'psycho' It will really be difficult for me to tell my family that I am going for mental counseling." (Asian female, age 27, 3rd year, single).

"No, because I don't think that it will be helpful. I rely on my family for counseling. I have not yet felt an urgent need to seek counseling elsewhere, probably because my parents are so supportive. I live with my family, so I don't have to suffer the difficulty of missing them, thank God." (Asian female, age 29, 3rd year, single).

"I don't need counseling because I am a strong person but FBSs should be given some opportunities and scholarships. We are treated like minorities." (North American male, age 28, 2nd year, single).

"I really don't have any mental problem as to think about going for mental counseling. I know how to deal with my stresses and anxieties that come from challenges of adjustment but not to think of going for counseling. I have never thought about it and I really don't think I need it." (South American female, age 21, 1st year, single).

"The only counselor I've ever been to was a transfer counselor. I didn't know what the best schools around here for FBSs are and she actually helped me a lot. It is different when you are a resident and it doesn't make much of a difference in price you pay, but being international and paying a triple amount forces you to choose what's affordable even though it may not be the school of your dreams." (European female, age 25, 2nd year, single).

"Counseling? I never think about that. But I think this can work when the people need it. Me, I did not come to this country forced, so if I have any problems I talk to my family. They are my best counselors and I know I can always go back to my home country if I see that I am not happy here any longer." (South American female, age 28, 2nd year, single).

"Tell you the truth, I don't need counseling because I solve my problems myself by exercising, meditation, concentration, studying, and talking to friends, I could have used a little help in the beginning when I walked into this country but that's over now." (Middle Eastern male, age 27, 3rd year, single).

"No, I never wanted to go for counseling because they don't understand us. I mean they won't understand our culture, my English and ways of life and so therefore will not know how to help me when I have problems. I normally call my parents or my godparents when I have problems and I still do even though I am now here in the US. My godparents have been giving me a lot of psychological support along with my parents since I came here. As a girl who is not married, I call my parents often because they want to know that I well protected here. They are like my life." (South American female, age 34, 3rd year, single).

Even though psychological disorientation was considered personal to individual FBS, participants in the focus group severally implicated language barrier as one of the major elements that exacerbate psychological disorientation as an offshoot of culture shock in the foreign-born students' psycho-cultural adjustment process. Some discussants seemed to be more interested in the attendant academic and classroom challenges while others seemed to be more focused on social challenges. For the most part, participants had a similar idea of the kind of challenges FBSs might be experiencing at the participating community colleges.

Interestingly, foreign-born student focus group members exhibited little or no interest in mental health counseling from the above responses. In general, there was this notion about mental health counseling as something either unnecessary or undesirable. Cultural values and principles that are suggestive of resilience and perseverance such as bouncing back, goal getter, and never give up attitudes or frames of mind in difficult life challenges seem to have been one of the major reasons that FBSs show little or no interest in mental health counseling. Some believe that self-effort and personal strength and determination through exercise, meditation, relaxation, concentration, studying and talking to their friends would help them solve any mental or emotional difficulties resulting from adjustment challenges. This is reflected in the responses from the only two male participants in the focus group discussions.

Several participants mentioned closeness to and support from their families as tremendously beneficial to their mental well-being during the period of adjustment as well as throughout their stay in college. From their reactions, and body language during discussions, there was a general sense that mental health counseling is something novel to some foreign-born students at the participating community colleges. There was no indication that their mental health condition would at any point get beyond their control or those of their family members and loved ones. Some believe that differences in cultural values would render going for mental health counseling ineffectual if at all necessary. It is significant to note that FBSs are more reserved than their host nationals and therefore would hardly open up unreservedly to anyone who is foreign to them. This is consistent with certain responses from two female participants during the deliberations:

> "In my country, people don't say anything to people who they don't know, but here people are free and sociable." (Asian female, age 29, 3rd year, single).

> "And I noticed that Indians are more reserved, whereas Americans are just kind of all out there." (Asian female, age 27, 3rd year, single).

Most participants felt that mental health counselors are fundamentally ignorant of their (FBSs') core cultural values and convictions. To some, it would be seem culturally outlandish and preposterous to think about going for mental health counseling considering their cultural assumptions and core family values. To some, it would be taboo and absurd to seek mental health counseling in a Western culture. This was eloquently expressed in the responses from the female participant from Asia:

> "....We don't really feel comfortable going for mental health counseling…My people, I mean my family, and friends, will laugh

in your face to hear that you are going for mental counseling. They will be looking at you as a 'psycho' It will really be difficult for me to tell my family that I am going for mental counseling." (Asian female, age 27, 3rd year, single).

(B) Cultural Inflexibility

This category captures foreign-born students' implicit views of themselves in the process of psycho-cultural adjustment to a new cultural milieu and lifestyle based on their experiences. Participants noted several cultural differences that appeared to affect their psycho-cultural adjustment at community colleges. Discussants described differences between the American peoples' ways of life and those of the FBSs as among the significant barriers to their social and interactional adjustment. They continued to describe their struggles to adjust better to the American culture and lifestyle. As their primary purpose in coming to the US was to be students, this challenge seems latently of great practical significance but not so much pronounced. Although participants mentioned a few differences in lifestyle, interests, and sense of pride, the few most striking points were gleaned from discussion excerpts slightly suggestive of cultural inflexibility and identity consciousness on the part of FBS discussants.

"I cannot change the way they (Americans) live. I just can make sure it doesn't become my lifestyle as well. My beliefs are more important to me and I live my life. I express what I think and if they want to accept it or not is their choice. I think that my problem is that I adapt to a new environment very fast and very well, and even though I say I don't like how these people rush through life forgetting about all these important things, I'm become like that too; that is my problem." (European female, age 25, 2nd year, single).

"I believe that Americans have a very different vision of the world. They seem to me different…….I don't have any problem but I don't agree with the vision of the world that Americans have. I still feel like an explorer and in constant moving." (South American female, age 28, 2nd year, single).

"Americans think that Brazilians live very intensely. I don't care, I'm like that and I won't change……No I don't feel like I am at home here because I have intrinsic family values that I hardly find on people born in this country. I am not pretentious to believe that I will become "one of them" but I also understand that this country is a melting pot. I do not think that the question is what can make me feel better. If I am not up to the challenges I should never had left my country. US is the way it is, I am the one who should adapt … I see people here are totally different from, my own people; all they do is about work and work and no more. But it's totally different in my country because there, people care for you but here people think that they are perfect." (South American female, age 28, 3rd year, single).

"This difference in culture sometimes creates a conflict within the school, within the church environment, because we are sometimes misjudged, sometimes criticized because of the way we see life." (North American female, age 34, 2nd year, married).

"Well, for me people in the Dominican Republic live their lives and enjoy it despite adversity. They are happy people by nature. We are happy people by nature. What I see here people live constantly under stress. People here worry too much. They think that little things are big things as opposed to not conform, but face it. We face problems but in a different approach. We do not always stress out in Dominican Republic. There is no need for that, if things can be so different." (South American female, age 31, 2nd year, married).

"I do agree with the previous responder. I feel that Americans are very…uptight…they have a very stressful lifestyle. Whereas I feel that like Indians are more lenient and buoyant in dealing with their lives…Indians are also more reserved, whereas Americans are just kind of all out there. I feel that just like other Asians, we Indians are more reserved than Americans." (Asian female, age 27, 3rd year, single).

"I respect all the cultures. And as well I will ask people to respect mine. What I miss from back home is my culture obviously, and some foods. I believe that I miss our food so much it's because no matter -- you try to cook the way they cook over there. For some reason it does not come the same way. And the culture too, because despite the fact that I had lived in Manhattan, previously where there's a lot of people from my country -- people don't relate to you the same as over there because people are too busy here (US). This country is about, you know, going, and going, and going and never stop. But it's totally different in my country because there people care for you but here people think that they are perfect… So that's why, I guess," (South American female, age 31, 2nd year, married)."

"Okay. Traditionally, we Koreans are more reserved than Americans, but this trend is changing in the present. Well, I think that my parents' generation of South Koreans was very old fashioned, and traditional as well as conservative. We have a rich cultural background, the older generations of my parents, that tend to see life in a more comprehensive way…Koreans are just as capitalistic, just as modernized, and there are many negative consequences and repercussions to that because, not every aspect of those ways of thinking and ideas is positive." (Asian female, age 29, 3rd year, single).

"Haitians strongly believe that the way to succeed, the way to advance in society is through education. There's no other way. It wasn't even an option. Your parents have pride in you as they see you excel. Haitians are also a hardworking people. We are hard working. My people believe that you have to take care of your family, you have to work. Respect especially for adults and for each other is also what we are known for. This includes not talking back to adults. Haitian kids would not talk back to an adult." (North American male, age 28, 2nd year, single).

"My West Indies (Trinidad) rearing taught me different values. West Indies' view and ways of life are very conservative compared to American people's way of life that is very liberal.

Our way of life is much more peaceful and slower." (South American female, age 21, 1st year, single).

"The main difference between the American and Korean culture is the respect shown to older people. I also find it challenging to understand the way many American students socialize, their views on intimate relationships (from my relatively conservative perspectives). On another note, I think, American people have more room in their mind and they willingly accept some happenings as their destiny. In my country, people don't say anything to people who don't know each other, but here people are free and sociable. The problem I have is that they are too open. It is comfortable to live here but sometimes I miss my family and my country's food. I mean I love it here but I prefer my country more." (Asian female, age 29, 3rd year, single).

It is expedient to mention at this juncture that the complexities involved in cultural inflexibility and identity consciousness became explicit in some discussants' descriptions of how they feel about cultural difference in relationship to their adjustment. Two female students from Europe and South America respectively at some point during the discussion clearly exhibited what sounded like cultural inflexibility and identity consciousness with the following statements: "Americans think that Brazilians live very intensely. I don't care, I'm like that and I won't change." "I cannot change the way they (Americans) live. I just can make sure it doesn't become my lifestyle as well. My beliefs are more important to me and I live my life." These discussants' spontaneous illustrations are quite insightful as well as provided a holistic view of what the above two psycho-cultural concepts (cultural inflexibility and identity consciousness) variously imply. Aside from FBS participants' responses, the dichotomy between the American peoples' lifestyle and those of foreigners were also highlighted by individualism and collectivism as much as by liberalism and conservatism palpably evident in the above responses.

Family Attachment and Academic Maladjustment
(A) Family Attachment

The above sub-construct seems to sum up the perspectives of the participants as regards deep family connections (family attachment). This sentiment was expressed in terms of foreign-born students missing family and home so much. One of the participants described contact with family as helping her reconnect to her roots as well as comforting her while having been far away from home. Typical family contact for FBSs is a very big source of moral and emotional support. Most of the participants in the focus group session do not have families here in the US. Remarkably, a female participant from Europe described in detail how much she misses her family and all the things associated with home. Similarly, another female from South America also shared with the group the extent to which she misses her own family and now always connects with them over the internet.

> "My family is small but we have a very close relationship. My husband and my two little children are all here. My mother and father are in the Dominican Republic. I talk to them with my little family here. I do my best to support my parents, my brothers and a sister down home. I do well to call them every week. Calling them really gives me some strength and energy when things get

tough here. Talking to them is very refreshing but I also have my little family here." (South American female, age 31, 2nd year, married).

"I love my family and I could not imagine my life without talking to them. I look forward to every summer to see them. I feel it (seeing them) is like a reward of the hard work throughout the year. If it comes to the things that I miss from home that I don't have here it is definitely my family. I see them only once a year in the summer when I go home. I love to spend time with them. I love the polish food we cook together with my mom. I try to cook polish dishes here too, but somehow it is not the same. If it is not for the ingredients, then it is the company. Nothing feels better than having a meal with your family. I think if my family was able to come and visit me once a while, it would make a big difference." (European female, age 25, 2nd year, single).

"I miss my family a lot. I was always with my family but not now (anymore). We used to talk every dinner. We talked small things to big issues; anything at all. Actually, I often keep contact with my family by internet service, so when I call them, actually it is similar with calling to a near friend." (South American female, age 28, 3rd year, single).

"No, I don't miss my family because they are here with me. I am always with my family. We talk every dinner. We talk small things to big issues; anything at all. I don't have to contact my family by internet service, or by phone calls. The relationship is stronger than ever before since I came to this country. We communicate every day. I feel very good being with them here. Communicating with them every day helps me a lot. It makes me feel better." (Asian female, age 29, 3rd year, single).

"I do miss family, but not to the extent that it is debilitating. I miss them because they make me laugh, they keep me grounded and they remind me of where I came from. My mother calls every few days so I am able to speak to them often. Facebook also allows me to keep in touch with my cousins. I enjoy talking to them because it's comforting." (Asian female, age 27, 3rd year, single).

"That's a good question actually. I miss my family because Haitian parents, even no matter how old you are, they will support you until you can get on your feet. They're not just going to kick you out. I call once a week. And that's what would keep me going. And when things would get tough in school, and that's where I would get my encouragement, looking to my other siblings and talking to my parents. And that, for me, was the drive, and also and that makes me not to take for granted, even things, if things get harder, and then get tough at times, to keep going, because there's a purpose. There is a reason why we are doing it. So, the family, my family, they the ones who keep me grounded and provide the support. And they're still going to be there, no matter how old you are, even if you're married and you have kids, you still have that close relationship with them." (North American male, age 28, 2nd year, single).

"One thing I discovered is that the farther away you are from home, the less you will get to see your family. I travel back home to see my family once every year but I do call them on the phone at least two times a week. It costs me to travel back home as well as talk to them every week, but that's okay because I need to be talking to them anyway and would wish to see them often." (South American female, age 21, 1st year, single).

"I really do miss my family. I miss them every day, but I am used to that feeling. Nowadays it is different though than it used to be. When I first came here I spent fortune on calling cards to be able to talk to them. I called them as much as I could and there was never enough. Now with Skype, cheaper ways of calling on the cell phone I talk to them almost every day. I go home for summer every single year for at least about a month. So, I always know that the time is coming as soon as the spring semester is over. However, there are times I miss them more than ever. Mostly when things get hard and stressful I really need them and Skype doesn't help much. I need their closeness and feeling they are there with me. I practically just answered this question. I love my family and I could not imagine my life without talking to them. I look forward to every summer to see them. I feel it is like a reward of the hard work throughout the year." (European female, age 25, 2nd year, single).

"I love my family and this should answer the question. We have a very close relationship. I talk to them several times a week. I feel like talking to them because they are my best friends. I miss my family a lot because we've always been a very close family. Any decision that I have to make in my life, my family is the first to know. I have conversation with them by phone. I talk with my parents every day and another people from family (sister, grandmothers) once a week. I love to talk to them, I feel very good and close to them." (South American female, age 28, 2nd year, single).

In response to the question: So, do we all agree that relationship with family helps us to adjust psychologically in a different environment, right? Almost all the participants chorused in unison: "Yes, yes, yes, absolutely, absolutely." This surprisingly happened almost in a rhythmically organized fashion. Interestingly other participants involved in the discussions were equally strongly in agreement with the comments of the previous respondents. There was no mixed picture regarding family influence in relation to family attachment and home nostalgia. In summary, they all agreed that relationship with family exerts enormous influence toward a positive psychological well-being of foreign-born students during their adjustment period. This finding is consistent with the quantitative study where we had conceptualized family attachment and home nostalgia as key components of FBSs' psycho-cultural adjustment challenges.

In this phase of discussions, I discovered that families come in different shapes and sizes as well as operate in different patterns. Most of the foreign-born students in focus group session referred not only to their parents and siblings as family members but also to uncles, cousins, nieces and nephews, grandparents, kinsmen and women and even their godparents. So, most of the references of FBSs to family members are not restricted only to their nuclear families (parents and siblings). One of the things impressively educative in this study is that the level of influence a family exerts on an individual FBS depends on the degree of relationship that exists between the FBS sojourners and their families. Also, the nature and level of influence families exert on their loved ones away from home is anchored on certain intrinsic family values. Such values take the form of education from childhood, sense of community, generosity, caring, nurturing, happiness, cheerfulness, hope, optimism, resilience, and courage. I gleaned these values from FBSs' responses to various questions on the focus-group discussions schedule. Interestingly, these intrinsic values, whatever their forms and cultural bases, carry with them a sense or feelings of affection, trust, security, fear reducing attachment, loneliness, potential despair, and anxiety among FBSs.

Some focus group respondents believed that hearing the voice, seeing the face, or even experiencing the physical presence of a family member in times of adjustment crisis was emotionally and psychologically reassuring. These interactions also augmented the foreign-born students' sense of self-confidence. We can see the evidence for this reflected in the following statements:

> "I really need them and Skype doesn't help much. I need their closeness and feeling they are there with me. I practically just answered this question. I love my family and I could not imagine my life without talking to them." (European female, age 25, 2nd year, single).

> "I am always with my family. We talk every dinner. We talk small things to big issues; anything at all. I don't have to contact my family by internet service, or by phone calls. The relationship is

> stronger than ever before since I came to this country. We communicate every day. I feel very good being with them here." (Asian female, age 27, 3rd year, single).

Such relationships with family members also go a long way to assuaging painful feelings and strengthen resilience in the face of adjustment difficulties.

(B) Academic Maladjustment

The majority of the focus group discussants made interesting observations that strongly diminish the impact of academic maladjustment as one of the major components of foreign-born students' psycho-cultural adjustment challenges at community colleges. They generally agreed that education and the academic system in the US is flexible, easier, less tedious, fun, and more practical. The active participatory aspect of students' involvement in class discussions was broadly highlighted in the US system of education by the interviewees. A female discussant from South America revealed that one of her major academic challenges was the realization of how less intimidated students appear in the classrooms here in the US. She further revealed how much time it took her to get fully adjusted to the fact that American faculty no longer seem unapproachable and noticeably authoritarian as obtainable in her home country. Her thoughts were encapsulated in the following statements:

> "I think my number one academic challenge was the style of teaching. We were taught to not challenge your teachers growing up." (South American female, age 21, 1st year, single).

She hinted that transition from British to American spoken and written English Language methodology also constituted a challenge but not intractable. These points
were further elaborated in *nitpicky* details below from individual participant's perspectives. Discussants from Asia, Latin America, Europe, Middle East, and North America aired their views on this very subscale (academic maladjustment):

"Well, all of this has to do with our kind of education back home. We have a free and compulsory primary and secondary education system back home. You are free to go to any school you like; public, private and religious schools. You can also go to college anywhere you choose. We have places where they teach people foreign languages. I found out that corporal punishment for students' misbehaviors down home has a different meaning here. A teacher can be thrown into prison here in America for flogging a student as a corporal punishment; I mean in the primary and secondary schools here. There are not many differences between the academic systems both here in the US and that of the Dominican Republic. The only big academic challenge in this country is the language but I was prepared and attended an English Language school before coming to the US because the language of instruction in the Dominican Republic is Spanish. Education is one of the values my parents instilled in me. They told me that we have the oldest University in the Americas. I was never afraid of studying in the US. I do not have problems in classes here in the US, only English Language was my problem at the beginning but now it is over." (South American female, age 31, 2nd year, married).

"I notice that school in India is more rigorous. There is also more discipline there than we have here in the US. In the US, though, there is too much work and not enough time for studies. The answer is not to give more work. There is rigid education system in India with strict discipline. In India, you cannot move from Law into Engineering. But, I have discovered that the US has a flexible system that will enable you to take any course any time as well as jump from one program into another." (Asian female, age 27, 3rd year, single).

"In my country (South Korea), students are more passive in class. We were quite individuals in the class, less talking but in here I have to be more involved in the classroom discussions. Everyone is active and participate in class. Students can speak. I love it. We have longer hours for class and the teachers have the passion to teach. Down home, we were pushed to study hard and go to good college but here it is free. Here I have a lot of work in the day time, so it is hard to concentrate on both things well. I think that in my country there is a strong educational environment." (Asian female, age 29, 3rd year, single).

"One thing that in high school that I was disappointed about, even though when I was in Haiti I was always on top of my class, and then I came here because the standards were different. So, the average in Haiti was combined with my grades here. And because of that I wasn't able to go to the schools that I dreamed of going.

So that was a big disappointment for me (North American male, age 28, 2nd year, single).

"I think my number one academic challenge was the style of teaching. We were taught to not challenge your teachers growing up. In college you were able to voice American and British ways of spelling and writing frequently confused my opinions and views. Because our school system was governed under the British Regime, the academic system in my country was very comprehensive and geared towards advanced tiered learning. In this country (US), there is a lot of remedial and basic learning. I thought all first year college courses were very easy. Yes, also there is less bureaucratic red tape to cut through. Education is highly regarded and valued in Caribbean and European countries thus use this as strategic plans to get ahead." (South American female, age 21, 1st year, single).

"I think that education in Poland is very good in a way we learned pretty much everything. There was no such a thing as choosing what you want to study in high school. When I hear college students saying they took or didn't take something in high school I never knew what they meant. We had to take everything with no exceptions. I think school in Poland and most Poland is much harder than it is here. However, it is harder in a bad way. I feel I had to study everything and it didn't really matter if I understood it or not. I memorized most of the things, took the test and two weeks later forgot what I learned. Probably the only barrier I still have sometimes is the language. After all, English is my second language and it sometimes makes it harder to understand things especially when you are a science major. I think the way they teach here is so much more practical. The only things I feel are unnecessary are giving kids too many ways of let's say multiplying and they get even more confused. Anyway, I feel the way teachers approach teaching kids here is so much better than in my country. Sometimes they are a bit too much, though. I just wish it wasn't so hard and expensive to be able to go to college here. Just the prices of the books are already ridiculous not mentioning the tuition. There are so many smart kids out there that are not able to pursue their dreams and show their talent because they can't afford going to school. I feel it is more interesting and fun to study here." (European female, age 25, 2nd year, single).

"I believe educations for kids are different than education for adults in this country so I am unable to answer this question because I did not study here when I was a child. I believe I can say from what I have seeing that kids in this country seem to have much less social life and much more responsibilities with schedules than back in my home country. I believe I did not have problems besides facing the prejudice of two professors in all my 4 years of school. Yes, there are differences. I believe I was better taught and the academic process was much more rigorous. I feel like I learned much more back home than in the USA. I have done 1 year college in my home country before transferring to the USA." (South American female, age 28, 2nd year, single).

"The system of education is quite different here. Well, English language was an issue in the beginning, but not anymore. The education system was very good there I have scored 100 percent in math but about 70 in English when I came to this country. I find it very easy to get an A in this country than my home country. No problems, the only problem I have had as I mentioned before was the fact that I was lacking in English language in the beginning but now everything is perfect. It is true that the education and academic system in my country... is strong, I will say; but there is nothing very exciting about it. Everything is religion based...Religion in my country affects everything. Here in America there is freedom of everything including education for everybody; both for boys and girls, as well as for men and women. It is not the same in my country. I am a man and a Christian but I feel bad about the discrimination against women when it comes to education in my country. They don't have equal freedom to get education as men do. In many colleges, men are only needed to teach men in class while women are required to teach only women in their class. Women are mostly not allowed to do some programs ... I used to feel that I am still in my country but not anymore. It's gone." (Middle Eastern male, age 27, 3rd year, single).

"In Ecuador, we have a well-established education system. Primary education has been compulsory and to some extent free too. Our education is compulsory until at least the age of 14. As kids we began primary education at the age of 6 and finished at the age of 12. We had two stages of secondary with each stage lasting for 3 years. All schools teach in Spanish. Overcoming language here in the US was the major problem and difference for me because here that I had to go to English Language classes to be able to attend classes here at the community college." (South American female, age 28, 3rd year, single).

From the focus group discussions, there was not any serious evidence that academic maladjustment was a major psycho-cultural adjustment challenge. Rather, it appears to be an offspring of difficult transition to a completely new academic culture. However, the issue of understanding the American teachers' accent was raised by a Jamaican female respondent, who complained about her difficulty getting over the American accent during class lectures and how she ultimately overcame this challenge. This researcher also discovered that the preceding reported adjustment challenge and its related psycho-cultural drawbacks in communication are mostly linked to different people's ways of speaking, listening and, above all, to both their paralinguistic and psycholinguistic make-up in pronunciations. This problem makes is difficult for FBSs to capture the rhythms and speed of speech from American professors. I discovered that many FBSs may have failed examinations simply because they were not able to clearly understand American professor's English speaking accent as well as those of their host peers and, therefore, demonstrably slow to follow lectures and class discussions that would enable them to pass their exams successfully. Participants vastly considered language barrier a major impediment in the academic transition from their various countries into the US. This researcher noted that FBSs from countries with English language speaking background have less difficulty in adjustment. Surprisingly, some respondents revealed that their countries have a comparatively good education and academic system some of which could rival the US system. There was an agreement that the US system is high but flexible, fun and less rigorous unlike what are obtainable in India that is more rigorous and inflexible and South Korea where the professors are the all-in-all in class with the students passive and non-participatory and in Poland where students do not necessarily have the freedom of choice in coursework. These statements testify to these facts:

> "I notice that school in India is more rigorous. There is rigid education system in India with strict discipline. You cannot move from Law into Engineering. I have discovered that the US has a flexible system that will enable you to take any course any time as well as jump from one program into another." (Asian female, age 27, 3rd year, single).

> "In my country, students are more passive in class. We were quite individuals in the class and less talking. But here I have to be more involved in the classroom discussions. Everyone is active and participates in class. Students can speak. I love it. But I think that in my country there is a stronger and stricter educational environment." (Asian female, age 29, 3rd year, single).

> "There was no such a thing as choosing what you want to study in high school. When I heard college students saying they took or didn't take something in high school I never knew what they meant. We had to take everything with no exceptions." (European female, age 25, 2nd year, single).

Responses from the participants strikingly point toward a more active participatory nature of class engagement in the US contrary to what is obtainable in most of the countries, whose FBSs' psycho-cultural adjustment challenges are being studied. A foreign-born student from a non-participatory academic culture will most likely find it difficult to adjust to a *participatory* academic system with facility. This type of presumed academic "deficiency" might potentially constitute some *nuisance* and a source of frustration to either the professor or a class discussions' peer group simply because the subject is probably grappling with troubled waters in a comparatively unfamiliar academic terrain. Non-performance in this aspect of academic adjustment may not be an objective indication of the student's true academic status or level of brilliance, but is definitely a major challenge to overcome; especially, a type that is based on a longstanding accumulation of different academic values and orientations.

In order to further understand what the issue of school "discipline" would mean, a response from a female respondent from South America revealed that her country employ corporal punishment for students' and pupils' misbehavior as applicable to some other foreign countries. These are the excerpts of her remarks:

> "I found out that corporal punishment for students' misbehaviors down home has a different meaning here. A teacher can be thrown into prison here in America for flogging a student as a corporal punishment; I mean in the primary and secondary schools here (South American female, age 31, 2nd year, married)."

Even though corporal punishment is not widely practiced here in the US, it is probable that a certain "flashback" or "carry-over" of such disciplinary school culture and mentality could influence FBSs' comportment in class as well as their overall psycho-cultural adjustment at the CCs. This type of negative mental transference of teacher-student relationship back home; where corporal punishments are practiced, could as well influence professor-student relationship at the community college levels and even beyond.

From the trajectory of the focus group discussions, majority of the participants seemed to believe in a more comprehensive and elaborate type of education in their home countries with a certain lack of depth in comparison to what is obtainable in the US. This showed up not only in the existing academic creativity, diversity and flexibility of program choice in the US but also in different academic standard *surprises* as agreed upon by the participants. Among those responses, the female respondent from Europe and the male respondent from North America made the following remarks:

"I think school in Poland and most Poland is much harder than it is here. However, it is harder in a bad way. I feel I had to study everything and it didn't really matter if I understood it or not. I memorized most of the things, took the test and two weeks later forgot what I learned." (European female, age 25, 2nd year, single).

"When I was in Haiti I was always on top of my class, and then I came here because the standards were different. So, the average in Haiti was combined with my grades here. And because of that I wasn't able to go to the schools that I dreamed of going. So that was a big disappointment for me." (North American male, age 28, 2nd year, single).

Overall, it is evident from the above discussions that participants noted some degree of distinctions between the US academic system and those they were used to in their various countries of origin. However, they did not observe significant differences in FBSs' academic adjustment as such as to potentially make achieving success in school an extremely stressful experience.

Interaction among Constructs and FBSs' Adjustment Progress

There seem to be complex interactions among cultural inflexibility, identity consciousness, and psychological disorientation that specifically inhibit foreign-born students' psycho-cultural adjustment at the community colleges in the US, thus creating some distance between both entities (the guests and the host). However, some of the ten (10) foreign-born student discussants indicated that they were able to break through cultural norms of passivity to foster adjustment, relationship, socialization and communication, thereby bridging the gap. The following stories illustrate these interactions and the various ways FBSs responded either by crossing the barrier, bridging the gap or not.

"One of my greatest challenges was getting to know American students at school. Having to go through the experience of knowing everyone was a little difficult especially in a different environment, language and way of life. But I relate well with the ones I know. I try to do so and just be nice to everyone." (North American female, age 34, 2nd year, married).

"Yes, I do get along with every American I have met. I can't complain and I try not to do so. I built some relationships with those of them who tried to come close to me. There are some of them who want to know about other cultures. I can say that I relate well with them, yes." (South American female, age 31, 2nd year, married).

"I think that I succeeded in relating well with Americans because I had to become more of an outgoing person by working to create relationships beginning with those of them I meet in class because I figured that was something I will use for life." (Asian female, age 27, 3rd year, single).

"Yeah....I relate well to Americans mostly. I have also made the effort over the years living here to understand their culture better. Yes, I do relate with Americans well but sometimes not. I think that the difference both in culture and lifestyles is the problem. I certainly do relate better with those who get to know me and my way of life. What makes relationship a bit difficult is that they seem a lot to be ignorant about my country and my culture and some of them do not appear to be interested to know." (Asian female, age 29, 3rd year, single).

"I think that I relate well with Americans because I am beginning to connect better with their ideas, values and lifestyles. I have even made a lot of friends who appreciate my views about things and they feel happy discussing about the world with me." (North American male, age 28, 2nd year, single).

"Yes, I try to relate well with them but I think that Americans probably consider me more of a person from Trinidad than an

American and that makes relationship with them a little difficult. I think that what makes a little difficult for me to relate better with some of them is….languages, discrimination, stereotyping. They also feel that they are better than everyone." (South American female, age 21, 1st year, single).

"I don't have a hard time dealing with Americans or anybody else. I feel I can get along with anybody. However, I do have a different view of them than other people. I know quite a few very nice American people I met in class and school in general and I love to talk to them when I see them. However, I noticed that when we say that we should meet outside of school, it usually ends there. It is just talking whereas when I plan to go out with people from different countries it actually happens. I have a huge group of international friends and we love to meet from time to time and spend hours having coffee and chatting. With my American friends (there are exception of course) we always say we have to meet up, but it hardly ever happens and I feel it is because we are all busy and they have to find time for their own group of friends first. I'm not sure if I understand the question again, but I think that if Americans stopped rushing through their lives and chase after the "more" and the "best" all the time, they could actually open their eyes and see the beauty of life and of the rest of the world. They would understand what they are missing." (European female, age 25, 2nd year, single).

"Some of them do relate well with me. Usually the ones who have travelled abroad or lived with foreigners; I feel ok with them.

When I arrived here I was the one who did not understand their way of living. When it happens to me I try to make fun of the moment and show that the differences are actually something that I am proud of. I do relate well with Americans because I have been immersed in their culture for a long time and there is not much that surprises me coming from them. My relationship with them is not hard because I learned how to socialize under their standards." (South American female, age 28, 2nd year, single).

"This is not a hard one for me to answer. Of course, I relate well with Americans. The relationship with American people is stronger now than ever before since I came to this country. I get along with many of them but sometimes, I keep thinking if I have really left my country…where you have a lot of fear because of you are a Christian when you relate to other students in school. Honestly, I just like spending time with those Americans here that I feel close to. That's the way I feel." (Middle Eastern male, age 27, 3rd year, single).

"Yes, I do try to relate well with Americans because I believe that one of the most rewarding things in life is to get along with everyone any place no matter what challenges you have. I try to relate well with them because that will help to make me happy and well-adjusted in college." (South American female, age 28, 3rd year, single).

Summary

This sequential explanatory mixed method study primarily examined and analyzed survey responses of 382 FBSs from the following continents and global regions: Asia, Africa, Europe, Latin America, Middle East, and North America. The responses from 10 participants in a focus group session were also examined and analyzed. As the researcher I utilized a mixed method approach in data analysis which combined both quantitative and qualitative data in one study. Participant responses to the questionnaire that included adjustment items were classified by subscale analysis into a three-structure subscale. Key elements of demographic information provided by respondents to the survey items facilitated general quantitative analysis.

The information gathered from both the survey exercise and focus group discussions provided the material pertinent for this study. Analyses of the frequency tables on the three psycho-cultural subscales in this study found that foreign-born students at community colleges are more likely to be inclined to family attachment and academic maladjustment as well as to identity consciousness and home nostalgia than to psychological disorientation and cultural inflexibility. Overall, integrated findings on the post-migration psycho-cultural adjustment challenges of FBSs are relatively significant enough to be overlooked. Approximately 31% of FBSs in the survey study agreed to all the related items on the three subscales; 48% disagree to all the related items on the three subscales while 21% remained neutral.

It is important to note that I discovered some discrepancies, differences, and inconsistencies in the pattern of foreign-born students' responses to the subscales (psycho-cultural variables) when juxtaposed with their (FBSs') responses to similar variables at the focus group discussions. In some cases, data from the survey item responses were contradictory to similar item responses in the focus group discussions. However, the focus group session findings indicate that FBSs have great potential to be more likely inclined to family attachment and home nostalgia as well as to identity consciousness and cultural inflexibility than to psychological disorientation and academic maladjustment. Findings that emerged from the focus group discussions provide the necessary explanation and context in which previous survey result may be better understood. They provide a deeper and richer picture of the psycho-cultural adjustment challenges of FBSs as presented by the participants in their own words as much as possible.

An integration of both approaches assumes as well as reflects a certain level of post migration psycho-cultural adjustment struggles among foreign-born students enrolled in the participating community colleges. The overall result indicates that there were certainly some unmet psycho-cultural needs among foreign-born students that could, potentially and negatively affect their academic progress as well as general well-being at community colleges in the Northeastern US. Both the quantitative and qualitative data in this study were further amalgamated in the next chapter as the product of the participant selection model and an explanation of available quantitative data following a mixed method approach.

CHAPTER V
Discussion, Conclusions and Recommendations

Introduction

Analyses presented in the preceding chapter permit an attempt at contextualizing influential variables at play in the post-migration psycho-cultural adjustment challenges of FBSs in a new cultural environment at CCs in the US. This chapter is designed to present the final discussions, conclusions and recommendations on study with the model framework consisting of the following predictor variables and constructs: identity consciousness and home nostalgia (IC&HN); psychological disorientation and cultural inflexibility (PD&CI); family attachment and academic maladjustment (FA&AM). Results of the study are summarized and discussed within the context of the key research question and subsidiary questions associated with the research. Overall, there is one major research question and three subsidiary research questions.

Chapter one provided a contextual overview of current study beginning with foreign-born student's background, the context under which they are being studied, significance and rationale of study and their various adjustment challenges at community colleges based on psycho-cultural concepts. Chapter Two was organized into areas which identified the key literature, theories and conceptual components: Understanding the background of study on FBSs psycho-cultural adjustment challenges which presupposes international education and migration. Reviewing literatures, theories and concepts on IS adjustment challenges based on a given psycho-cultural framework. Chapter Three presented explanations of the methodology used and included descriptions of the pilot study, the survey instrument, the sample selection, data collection, data analysis and the general statistical procedures utilized. Chapter four contained detailed analysis of the data and presentation of findings using frequency tables with brief adjoining commentaries. FBSs' psycho-cultural adjustment challenges were examined via FBS responses to items that were designed the key components previously identified. The impacts of the demographic characteristics on FBSs' psycho-cultural adjustment were tested for statistical significance. ANOVA tests of Between-Subjects Effects were conducted using data from the 36 Likert-type subscale survey items that addressed demographics of FBSs at CCs in the Northeastern US. In addition to the discussions and limitations of study, a summary section and specific recommendations for future research brought the research project to a conclusion in this current chapter (Chapter Five). Following general study discussions, various recommendations were made for the development of a more effective and befitting adjustment environment for FBSs at CCs.

Purpose of the Research

The purpose of this research was to examine post-migration psycho-cultural adjustment challenges of foreign-born students at community colleges in the US. This investigation was guided by a conceptual rationale, research questions, and literature review. Its purpose is to determine whether FBSs experience some level of post-migration psycho-cultural adjustment challenges in a culture and environment that is new to them, to what extent and in what ways. In other words, this study is a helpful attempt at explaining, among others, why FBSs or immigrants could potentially remain psycho-culturally unsettled despite efforts to learn and follow the rules in a new culture and country of sojourn or immigration as suggested by various theories and concepts (Belozersky, 1992; Fritz, Chin, & DeMarinis,2008; Hofstede, Hofstede, & Minkov,2010; Kim,2002; Mishal & Morag, 2002; Oyserman, Coon & Kemmelmier, 2002; Ross, 2001; Triandis, 2002; Ward,2001). As indicated in the previous chapters, I as researcher used both quantitative and qualitative methods to shed light on the phenomenon of potential post-migration psycho-cultural maladjustment of FBSs at CCs in the US. This research sought to answer the following questions:

1. To what extent and in what ways do FBSs enrolled in CCs in the US face post migration psycho-cultural adjustment challenges?
2. To what extent in what ways do post-migration psycho-cultural adjustment challenges differ among groups of FBSs (such as gender, age, year in college, continent of origin, marital status and family presence) enrolled in CCs in the US?
3. To what extent and in what ways are post-migration psycho-cultural adjustment challenges related to the outcomes (Social Interaction and Academic/Career Engagement) of FBSs' adjustment at CCs in the US?

Data Collection

As at June 5, 2012, 382 usable questionnaires were received for a response rate of 44%. Most of the respondents; 69% (262) indicated that they are female while 31% (120) indicated that they were male FBSs of the participating CCs. In order to answer the above research questions, all the survey items were collapsed into the key items and constructs needed to address this research questions. This approach was employed to lessen the dominance of non-salient survey items. Responses were weighted by

FBSs' response rates using three emergent psycho-cultural domains or components (subscales A, B & C). The focus group session was conducted on June 27, 2012 with 80% (8) IS participants indicating that they were female while 20% (2) indicated that they were male. Guide questions of similar attributes were amalgamated into summary questions (items) to enable researcher get details from participants in a single shot. Data comprised qualitative responses of 10 participants from Asia, Latin America, Europe, Middle East and North America.

Various data categories and subcategories were identified following quantitative data analyses and a qualitative data analyses of a constant comparative method whereby line, sentence and paragraph segments of the transcribed discussions and written responses were reviewed to decide what codes fit the constructs suggested by the entire data (Krueger, 1994; Krueger & Casey, 2000; Strauss & Corbin, 1998). The patterns of relationship among the major components observed in this study provided support for the stability of the findings.

Summary of the Findings
Survey Data Analyses

In the empirical survey research part of this study, responses to the items on the three emergent subscales were intended to address the research questions listed above. Frequencies and the percentage item means relative to each subscale were used as a measure of the potential presence of psycho-cultural adjustment challenges among IS respondents. Therefore, responses to items on the three-factor subscales and scores were used as observed indicators of potential post-migration psycho-cultural adjustment challenges of FBSs at CCs. Scores of IS responses to items; both in agreement and in disagreement, were allowed to partial out across three component subscales. Inspection of the FBSs' response distribution shows that respondents to all the items on subscale A (first factor), labeled identity consciousness and home nostalgia; subscale b (second factor): psychological disorientation and cultural inflexibility and subscale c (third factor): labeled family attachment and academic maladjustment mostly disagreed or strongly disagreed to most of the items on the subscales. Contrary to researcher's expectations; hugely based on preliminary literature review, this result indicates a relatively low level of psycho-cultural adjustment challenges among FBSs. Besides, FBSs' average mean responses (2.76) to all the items on the entire thee-factor subscale, failed to meet the set midpoint level of interest of 3.0 or above to be considered important indicators of variable(s) support.

On a special note, with a singular consideration, responses to items on subscale C; depicted in Table 11, presented a different but remarkable scenario. Inspection of response distribution shows that respondents to all the items on this third component (subscale C), labeled family attachment and academic maladjustment, either agreed or strongly agreed to most of the items on the subscale. Moreover, FBSs' mean responses (3.24) to all the 10 items on the subscale exceeded the required midpoint level of interest of 3.0 to be considered important indicators of variable support. Results suggest that even though FBSs enrolled in CCs experience a comparatively low psycho-cultural adjustment challenges in relation to the identity consciousness and home nostalgia as well as psychological disorientation and cultural inflexibility aspects of the psycho-cultural adjustment phenomenon, the impact of family attachment and academic maladjustment remains prominent. Neutral responses, which constitute approximately 21% of average IS responses to all the items on the three subscales are of interest to this researcher since institutional management might need data for decision and policy making. Moreover, the validity of neutral opinions can be such that possible conclusions could be drawn from ambivalent opinions, and possible routes for further exploration. Therefore, neutral responses will not be overlooked in the final data discussions and conclusion.

Overall, this researcher found that survey respondents in this study reported relatively low levels of psycho-cultural adjustment challenges at CCs in the Northeastern United States. From the general responses, most respondents sounded as well as appeared approximately "well adjusted" psycho-culturally in their item choices. However, responses varied across the adjustment domains portrayed by the three subscales (A, B & C). These subscales were represented by Tables *9, 10 and 11* in the previous chapter.

To answer the subsidiary research question two, analysis of variance model (ANOVA) tests were used to determine the impact of the demographic subscales' impact on FBSs' psycho-cultural adjustment at CCs. One-way analyses of variance used across the three factor subscales. Gender was not found to be a statistically significance predictor of FBSs' psycho-cultural adjustment challenges at CCs. Age was found to be statistically significant only on subscales A and B ($p < .05$) but not statistically significant on subscale C ($p > .05$). ANOVA test out-puts indicated that marital status and year in college are both statistically significant in relation to subscale B ($p < .05$) but not statistically significant to subscales A and C ($P > .05$). Continents of origin was found to be statistically significant only in relation to subscale C ($p < .05$) but not statistically significant to subscales A and B ($p > .05$). Also, in relationship to subscale A, one-way ANOVA test indicated that family presence in the

US is statistically significant (.001 < .05) but not statistically significant to subscales B and C (p> .05).

Frequency and descriptive statistics utilizing means and standard deviations for FBSs' responses to both items 37 to 44 and selected items 34 to 36 on the survey instrument addressed subsidiary research question number three. To address this research question, a positive psycho-cultural adjustment outcome, associated to social interaction and academic/career engagement, was predicted on higher mean scores from FBSs who answered *yes* to related items as depicted in tables 18 and 19. Findings revealed that majority of FBSs answered yes to most of the related to positive outcome variable; indicating that potential psycho-cultural adjustment challenges did not have significant impact on their social interaction; especially, with American students, faculty members as well as on their continued desire for academic and career engagement in the US.

Focus Group Data Analyses

The focus-group discussions findings provided detailed insights into the thoughts, feelings and opinions of FBSs on their psycho-cultural adjustment challenges at CCs. This section summarizes the result of the focus group session. Information from the focus group discussions which cut across identity consciousness and home nostalgia; psychological disorientation and cultural inflexibility and family attachment and academic maladjustment emphasize the findings gleaned from the preceding survey research but rather expanded knowledge about the psycho-cultural concept of FBSs' adjustment challenges at CCs. Illustrative themes, ideas and patterns emerged that delineated FBSs' potential psycho-cultural adjustment challenges at CCs. In general, the focus group discussions portrayed certain feelings of identity consciousness and home nostalgia among FBSs as they consistently referred to their own people and culture during discussions. This compound construct (identity consciousness and home nostalgia) was evident in their general descriptions of their feelings about differences between their home culture and the host culture. This researcher also found that some IS participants exhibited certain verbal attitudes, while expressing feelings and thoughts about cultural differences that are not only suggestive of possible cultural inflexibility and psychological disorientation but also presuppose potential psycho-cultural maladjustment post migration.

Overall, participants were almost unanimously explicit on how much they miss their families as well as acknowledged certain differences in the academic system between their own countries and the US. This aspect of their responses implicated strong family attachment and a certain but relatively minor level of academic maladjustment. The focus group discussions certainly created a reliable forum where potential psycho-cultural adjustment challenges of FBSs at CCs were more conveniently exposed. The focus group discussions schedule is included in the appendix (see Appendix B).

Discussion of the Findings
Identity consciousness and home nostalgia

This study was principally concerned with examining post-migration psycho-cultural adjustment of foreign-born students at community colleges especially as related to identity consciousness and home nostalgia; psychological disorientation and cultural inflexibility as well as family attachment and academic maladjustment as the major influential factors implicated literature. According to the findings in this study, the identity consciousness and home nostalgia scale (subscale A) contributed 17.1% as well as captured next to highest frequency of FBSs' disagreeable responses to all the items on the entire scale. Moreover, the average response mean also failed to meet the required midpoint average score of 3.0. This finding indicates that this compound construct may not be considered an important predictor of post-migration psycho-cultural adjustment challenges of FBSs at CCs. This finding relatively disaffirms what might have been expected given the tendency for FBSs to hold tight to their self and group identities as much as communicate a nostalgic desire for home following certain experiences that stem from being away from their home countries (Marginson & Sawir, 2011; Rizvi, 2005). Also, this finding did not resonate with the focus group session findings in which majority of participants implicitly expressed identity consciousness, and explicitly admitted that they experienced some level of home nostalgia. However, participants acknowledged that this experience might be alleviated by a more positive and better acculturation in a new culture and environment.

In a similar vein, I identified statements from discussants that suggest some level of identity consciousness and home nostalgia among them, post migration. It is understandable because in the bulk of research in cross-cultural psychology, both self-identity and group identity are understood as constant because FBSs form themselves whereas trajectories between host country identity and home country's identity continues to evolve in their chosen country of education and sojourn. FBSs are normally seen more as self-formed than 'adjusted.' Consistent with the result of this research as well as with previous other studies (Marginson & Sawir, 2011; Rizvi, 2005; Ward, Bochner & Furnham,

2001) for many FBSs, one or more elements of self-identity are seen as relatively fixed and slow to change. Such elements are linked to familial relations, or cultural or national identity, or language or first use or memories defined as 'home' or 'the true I.' Therefore, this compound subscale of identity consciousness and home nostalgia seems to relatively constitute a part of the primary issues that indicate psycho-cultural maladjustment among FBSs at the participating CCs. FBSs' responses to the identity consciousness and home nostalgia subscale may have further explanations for the reasons FBSs would not seek psychological or emotional help from a college-appointed or hired counselor but would rather seek academic help, from a guidance counselor instead, to avoid losing 'face' (academic identity). In fact, one of the focus group participants revealed that the only counselor she had ever seen was an academic guidance and transfer counselor. This type of attitude from FBSs could be partly attributed to certain levels of identity consciousness details of which were revealed during the focus group session.

In response to the suggestions: "I don't feel like myself in this country" and "I often feel having lost the ways of life of my family and other things we like in the family," which have to do with self-identity, totals of 72.2% (276) and 57.3% (219) FBSs disagreed to both items respectively; indicating that majority of IS respondents feel that they have not really lost their self-identity but instead are conscious of it. Contrary to the survey findings, the trajectory of the focus group discussions indicates that majority of FBSs are very conscious of both their self and group identity. At least 7 out 10 of them spoke passionately about longing for their homes and countries of origin, 3 provided details regarding their self and group identity while 5 respondents explained at length how much they miss their various homes.

Expectedly, on the home nostalgia subscale, the survey data findings indicated that FBSs agreed overwhelmingly to the item: "Talking to my family on the phone will always make me feel better." Of those foreign-born students responding, 60.7% (232) of 382 agreed that talking to their family on the phone would always make them feel better; 47.6% (182) did not feel like talking to their family every day; while 43.7% (167) indicated that even though majority of FBSs would like to keep a positively constant contact with their families, a significant percentage do not worry a lot about their families back home. Since a predominant fraction of FBSs, 69% (264) indicated that they had family here in the US, it is most likely that international student responses to the above last two items linked to home nostalgia may have been impacted by the presence of their families in the US.

Psychological Disorientation and Cultural Inflexibility

Results from the present study indicated that the psychological disorientation and cultural inflexibility scale (subscale B) contributed 9.6% to the total variance as well as captured the highest frequency of FBSs' disagreeable responses to all the items on the entire scale. Moreover, it was found that the average mean of FBSs' responses to all the items failed to meet the set midpoint average score of 3.0. Therefore, this variable may not be considered an important predictor of FBSs' psycho-cultural challenges at CCs. This finding stands in contrast to what might have been expected given relatively more stressful environments at CCs that often flow from a quite overwhelming experience of primarily living in a new culture with anticipated dissimilarities between home culture and host culture aside from their (FBSs') strong tendency to cling to their cultural identity (Barletta & Kobayashi, 2007; Hofstede, Hofstede,

& Minkov, 2010; Kim, 2002 & Neuliep, 2006). This finding is especially not consistent with the focus group findings in this present study where majority of participants agreed that they experienced some level of psychological disorientation after migration but acknowledged that this experience was only temporary. Participants believed that coping skill largely depended on individual person's mindset. I identified statements and in some cases frustration-ridden remarks from focus-group discussants, that suggest exhibitions of potential for cultural inflexibility post migration. This could find deeper cultural and better psycho-cultural interpretations in the works of Hosftede (2000) and Trompenaars & Hampden-Turner (1998). Their findings, theoretical notions and the details of the distinctions they made between societal deep cultural values such as individualism versus collectivism (communitarianism); universalism *versus* particularism; and achievement versus ascription orientations may not only serve to distinguish between societies and cultures but also offer insightful explanations to FBSs' perceptions and frustrations about their previously unspoken conflicts in cross-cultural relationships. On one hand, individualism, universalism, and achievement-orientated cultural values to which the US ascribes lay more emphasis on independence, autonomy, personal accomplishments, and abiding by the laws as well as rules than on friendships and relationships (Hofstede, 2000; Trompenaars & Hampden-Turner, 1998). Like the US, societies that value individualism, universalism and achievement-oriented "psycho-cultural" assumptions as their modus operandi as well as modus vivendi would most likely have citizens and nationals that give precedence to their personal tasks, works, lawful regulations, and personal achievements to enable them secure a good standing in the society over establishing friendships and relationships that they perceive have little to contribute towards their future successes in both academics and personal life careers. On the other hand, collectivism, particularism, and ascription-orientated "psycho-cultural" values lay more emphasis on dependence, interdependence, obligations of relationships and friendships, as well as group solidarity than on legal codes and regulations (Hofstede, 2000; Trompenaars & Hampden-Turner, 1998). Likewise, societies that value collectivism, particularism, and ascription-oriented assumptions both as their modus operandi and modus vivendi to which most of the FBSs studying in the US belong, would most likely have citizens and nationals that give precedence to dependence, interpersonal relationships, respect for individual social statuses and values, group loyalty, friendships, and personal connections that will enable them secure a good standing as well as establish a sense of belonging in the society over strict observance of rules, laws and regulations that they perceive do not have much to contribute towards their well-being and general subsistence. In line with the preceding analyses, a female FBS respondent from South America revealed that people from her country are, generally, dependent and consult one another, especially family members, close relations, and elders, in order to get their opinions on certain issues that are of paramount importance to them. Variations among these cultural assumptions, as described above, would certainly offer deeper and clearer explanations to most of the FBSs' post-migration psycho-cultural adjustment challenges that found expressions and hearing during the focus group discussions. Understandably, such deep-rooted differences in cultural orientations and values; if not properly moderated, could exacerbate or rekindle bicultural conflicts as well as aggravate potential intolerance in the form of cultural inflexibility, as well as identity consciousness, home nostalgia and their attendant psychological disorientation especially on the side of the immigrants or sojourners.

Additionally, and consistent with the preceding suggestions, Trompenaars and Hampden-Turner (1997) found that people from opposing cultural orientations are most like to perceive each other with some kind of distrust during social interactions. This type of attitudes and predispositions, might potentially impact the parties' cross cultural as well as interpersonal relationships. Therefore, statements such as, "… This country (US) is about, you know, going, going and going and never stop. But it is totally different in my country because there, people care for you but here people think that they are perfect…;" "Unfortunately, I feel that American people are not open minded. I feel they think this is the best country in the world…;" "Americans think that Brazilians live very intensely. I don't care, I'm like that and I won't change." "I cannot change the way they (Americans) live. I just can make sure it doesn't become my lifestyle as well" and "My beliefs are more important to me and I live my life," should not be misconstrued by researchers, FBS directors, advisors, counselors, caseworkers, and therapists as necessarily signs of aggression or dislike for the host nation but may inversely find a better psycho-culturally contextual analysis based on the previously discussed studies conducted by Hostede (2000); Trompenaars and Hampden-Turner (1997) and Trompenaars and Hampden-Turner (1998). Expectedly, some of these preceding statements; gleaned from the FBSs' focus group discussions, may have been taken as clear indicators of FBSs' possible cultural inflexibility deeply rooted in ethnocentrism, as well as help sensitize counselors and therapists to the potential presence of FBSs' psycho-cultural maladjustment propensity. However, it should also be noted that the predictive capacity of this type of respondents' variable may not have been particularly very strong as it seems especially when applied to all FBSs at the US CCs. Nevertheless, this finding remains interesting as well as intriguing. Regarding predominantly disagreeable responses to items linked to the psychological disorientation subscale, it is possible that FBSs may have developed a certain psycho-cultural resilience as well as made significant improvements in their acculturative skills in response to extraordinary stresses in their new social and cultural environment. This possible trend may have resulted in low levels of both psychological disorientation feelings and display of cultural inflexibility in cross-cultural adaptation among FBSs, given their responses to items associated with the related subscales.

Moreover, low levels of FBSs' responses to the psychological disorientation and cultural inflexibility subscale may partly have offered explanations for their low recognition of the importance of psychological counseling at their CCs. This view, which was most prevalent among the focus-group discussions' respondents, is consistent with the findings of Nilsson, Berkel, Flores & Lucas, 2004, Lin and Yi, 1997, Khoo, Abu-Rasain, & Hornby, G., 2002, Mori, 2000; and Nilsson and Anderson, 2004. Their findings suggest that many FBSs feel reluctant to share their feelings or emotions, express their opinions or oppositions to anyone, especially, authority figures. This is, probably, as a result of their stereotypical quietude, reserved attitude and non-assertive dispositions as culled from this present study.

Suffice it to remark that in the previous studies, utilizing counseling services might have been viewed as appropriate for only "crazy" people and reticence in this connection may also have been linked to cultural taboos that discountenance sharing private or family information with strangers (Nilsson, Berkel, Flores & Lucas, 2004; Lin &

Yi, 1997; Khoo, Abu-Rasain, & Hornby, G., 2002; Leong & Chou, 2002; Martinez, Huan, Johnson & Edwards, 1989; Mori, 2000). This type of attitude from FBSs could be appropriately ascribed to certain levels of cultural inflexibility, psychological disorientation and identity consciousness engendered by separation from their own people, the stigma that their culture may attach to mental health counseling and the drive to keep their self and cultural identity sacrosanct. Researcher further discovered that these psycho-cultural maladjustment indicators, when not properly tamed, often inspire some level of fear, guilt, frustration, a feeling of shame, insecurity and mistrust in them (FBSs) against sharing with outsiders or strangers exclusively personal issues. This finding diminishes the probability of FBSs utilizing psycho-cultural counseling. The direction of FBSs' responses in the focus group discussions, indicated that it is only on extreme situations, that FBSs would attempt to seek mental health counseling; it would take them a very long time to make such decisions if at all probable. Surprisingly, the survey data findings, in this study, indicated that of 382 international student participants 70.4% (269) of IS respondents disagreed to this suggestion: "people believing me to be crazy if they see me going for counseling." Similarly, 64.6% (247) of FBSs of 382 participants disagreed to statement: "I don't feel like visiting the counselor even when I have problems." Moreover, responses to those two suggestions failed to meet the set midpoint mean score of 3.0 or above to be considered important indicators of subscale support.

Focus group session respondents also signified their ability to successfully resolve their mental and emotional problems using their own inner power. Their responses support the findings of previous research which suggest that limited number of FBSs have utilized counseling services (Harju, Long & Allred, 1998; Nilsson, Berkel, Flores & Lucas,

2004). While survey findings contradict the findings of the same research, the focus group interview session in this research upholds the same previous research findings which observed that FBSs seldom availed themselves of psychological (mental health) counseling.

Family Attachment and Academic Maladjustment

Results from data analysis which provided strong support to family attachment as well as potential academic adjustment issues among FBSs enrolled in the CCs, indicated that the family attachment and academic maladjustment scale (subscale C) contributed 7.4% to the total variance as well as captured the highest frequency of FBSs' agreeable responses to items on the subscale. An overwhelming majority of international student respondents agreed with 9 of 10 items on the subscale. Moreover, the average response mean also met the required midpoint average score of 3.0 or above and therefore considered important indicators of potential psycho-cultural adjustment challenges of FBSs at CCs.

An outstanding number of IS respondents to the survey questionnaire indicated that they miss their families in various ways. In this family attachment and academic maladjustment subscale are two surprising and particularly revealing responses. 41.9% (160) of FBSs equally agreed to the following items: "I do not always feel safe simply because I am away from home" and "I feel that I am not doing very well in class works because of my English." On the other hand, 36.4% (139) of FBSs disagreed to the former item while 31.2% (119) disagreed to latter item.

Aside from the survey data family attachment came atop of the emerging subscales during the focus-group discussions. This clearly reinforces the survey result which points towards missing family as the most influential reason of FBSs' psycho-cultural maladjustment because of certain intrinsic family values. It is notable from the focus group discussions that certain family values and norms have been instilled in FBSs and such make them see their families as indispensable in their personal and social life. FBSs not only owe commitment to them but also see themselves as owing loyalty to their families as well as put so much trust in them. Family bond was seen as a tangible life blood of their existence on earth. Therefore, they would always consult their families before taking any important decisions. They would also rely on them for emotional help and support. Respondents believe that attachment to family leads to greater academic effort. This is especially significant as the survey questionnaire analysis also supports this suggestion. Focus group respondents also admitted that family attachment somewhat constitutes some pooling effects to return home.

Hazen and Albert (2006) reported that about 78% of respondents in a focus group conducted on FBSs as visitors or immigrants mentioned that friends and family back home, proved to be, by far, the most common incentive for them to return home. Contrary to researcher's expectation that this response might be more common among women as well as among FBSs from Asia, African and South America, this response appeared popular across the board with no significant associations with gender, age, and marital status, year in colleges or continent of origin. However, it has not been established whether family attachment remains constant or changes overtime as FBSs become more acculturated to a new culture and environment.

Questions about academic maladjustment produced interesting results with the quality and quantity of responses to this item relatively high. Foreign-born students admitted contending with a different educational system that might require some study flexibility and social skills. Certain responses were indicative of the idea that FBSs strive to do well academically in order to live up to the expectations of family and friends back home. These findings replicate previous research which suggested that it would seem "disastrous" for an FBS (an international student) to return to his or her home with a poor degree, but not to get a degree altogether would be a "shame" almost too much to bear (Livingstone, 1960 as cited in Khoo, Abu-Rasain, & Hornby, 2002). There seem to be a significantly positive causation between academic difficulties and cultural maladjustment (Lin & Yi, 1997; Wan, Chapman, & Biggs, 1992). These researchers noted that FBSs found it very difficult to adjust to English Language and the educational system in the foreign country. For example, FBSs have difficulty adjusting to the various accents of the lecturer, along with their different styles, and they have difficulty in understanding lectures, which makes them feel reluctant to participate in class discussions (Lin & Yi, 1997; Wan, Chapman, & Biggs, 1992).

Foreign-born students from non-English speaking backgrounds find test construction and comprehension difficult, as they require extra time to read academic materials, write and process understanding as well as comprehension (Ryan & Tribal, 2000). In addition, due to their limited vocabulary, they are often unable to easily articulate their knowledge for assignments, exams or research papers (Lin & Yi, 1997; Wan, Chapman, & Biggs, 1992). For many FBSs, poor English skill could be a major stressor and can create significant problems and barriers when trying to succeed and function in a new academic culture and environment. Overall, academic and language difficulties are critical problems for FBSs as the expectation of high performance can often bring about depression or lack of confidence if these expectations are not met (Barletta & Kobayashi, 2007). In her reviews of FBSs in English-speaking universities, Andrade (2006) identified English language proficiency, culture, support services, and educational background as influential toward the academic achievement of FBSs. Several researchers have investigated how students' language proficiency in English language, affect their adjustment (Poyrazli, Arbona, Nora, McPherson & Pisecco, 2002; Swami, Arteche, Chamorro-Premuzic, & Furnham, 2009).

  It is striking to remark that most focus group discussants have a certain reservation and objection to their home countries' authority-based method of teaching and learning. However, they all expressed desire to participate actively and consciously in the learning process but with more positive attitudes to group collaboration in the exploration of academic materials. This finding corroborates the works of Andrade (2006) and Barletta and Kobayashi (2007) who noted that for foreign-born students, adjusting to university life is complicated as they need to learn and negotiate cultural issues first to have access to the academic, social and other resources at the university. For instance, in the US, it is expected that students should ask questions, whereas in many other cultures, it could be considered disrespectful to question a professor in class. Some FBS respondents succinctly confirmed this claim during the focus group discussions.

Conclusions from the Research Questions

This study investigated post-migration psycho-cultural adjustment challenges of FBSs at CCs in the Northeastern United States. It specifically examined the following psycho-cultural characteristics: identity consciousness and home nostalgia; psychological disorientation and cultural inflexibility; family attachment and academic maladjustment (Belozersky, 1990; Fritz, Chin, & DeMarinis, 2008; Mishal & Morag, 2002; Ross, 2001; Hofstede, Hofstede, & Minkov, 2010; Oyserman, Coon & Kemmelmier, 2002; Triandis, 2002).

Information was sought to determine to what extent and in what ways FBSs from various countries and continents face those psycho-cultural challenges and the level of impact challenges have on their academic and social life. Descriptive statistics, as well as ANOVA techniques were used for the quantitative data. In addition, a factor analysis was run on the collected data. Based on factor analyses, some items were collapsed and the number of components (domains) was reduced. Discussions were conducted in a focus group session among volunteer FBSs at the CCs. Their responses were instrumental to the conclusions drawn in this study. Research questions and subsidiary questions were addressed as follows:

Research Question 1: To what extent and in what ways do FBSs enrolled in CCs in the US face post-migration psycho-cultural adjustment challenges?

This question was best addressed by all the items distributed across the three subscales (A, B & C) that constitute the one psycho-cultural adjustment scale. The survey part of this study found that FBSs enrolled in CC in the US face relatively very low psycho-cultural adjustment challenges.

FBSs' responses to items related to psychological disorientation and cultural inflexibility (PDCI) on subscale B; ranked last. These items on subscale B have a cumulative mean item agreement of 16.72% and a cumulative mean item disagreement of 62.86%. This means that approximately 17% of all FBS participants experience certain degrees of PDCI, after migration; approximately 63% disagreed to such experiences while about 20% remained neutral to the items on the PDCI subscale.

FBSs' responses to the items related to identity consciousness and home nostalgia (IOHN) on subscale A came next with a cumulative mean item disagreement of 49.75% and a cumulative mean item agreement of 29.58%. This means that approximately 50% of FBSs signified disagreement or strong disagreement to the items on the ICHN subscale; 30% of FBSs indicated that they experience certain degrees of ICHN; while about 20% average of FBSs remained neutral.

FBS responses to survey items related to family attachment and academic maladjustment subscale (FAAM) ranked first; with a cumulative mean item agreement of 47.98 % and a cumulative mean item disagreement of 26.34%. This means that approximately 48% of FBSs surveyed experience family attachment and academic maladjustment issues, post migration; approximately 26% of FBS respondents indicated disagreement or strong disagreement while about 26% maintained neutrality in response to items on the FAAM subscale.

An examination of the survey results based on the above three subscales (A, B & C), indicates that the primary factor influencing FBSs' post-migration psycho-cultural adjustment at CCs is family attachment and academic maladjustment (FAAM). Moreover, among the three subscales (A, B & C) that make up the psycho-cultural subscale, only the family attachment and academic maladjustment subscale (C) met the set midpoint average score of 3.0 or above to be considered important indicators of variable (subscale C) support. Besides, of 32 items denoting psycho-cultural tendencies across the three subscales, 10 captured higher percentages of FBSs' item agreement. The cumulative mean agreement to all the items on the three subscales (A, B & C) is 31.4%; while cumulative mean disagreement is 46.32%. 22.28% remained neutral. Based on the result of this survey, it could be empirically assumed that FBSs enrolled in CCs in the US face a relatively low level of psycho-cultural adjustment challenges.

Research Question 2: To what extent and in what ways do post-migration psycho-cultural adjustment challenges differ among groups of foreign-born students (such as gender, age, year in college, continent of origin, marital status and family presence) enrolled in CCs in the US?

This question was also measured by all the items distributed across the three subscales (A, B & C) that constitute the one psycho-cultural adjustment scale. This question is best answered by referring to the research and data analysis from FBSs' responses to the thirty four items that addressed this query.

Analysis of variance (ANOVA) test of between-subjects effects based of foreign-born students' responses to items on the three subscales (A, B & C), indicated that that FBSs' psycho-cultural adjustment is not influenced by gender. This implies that it made no statistically significant difference if an IS respondent was male or female. Therefore, gender has no statistical significance in relationship to FBSs' psycho-cultural adjustment at CCs in the US.

Foreign-born students' age influenced their PDCI and FAAM experience in responses to items on subscale A and C. This implies that FBSs' age range will make a statistically significant difference in their psycho-cultural adjustment at CCs. However, age did not have any statistical significance in their ICHN adjustment experience in responses to items on subscale A. In relation to scale A and C, a post hoc test (Tukey HSD) specifically indicated that FBSs within younger age groups of 18-25 and 36-45 are more likely to be impacted by identity consciousness and home nostalgia issues more than FBSs with the older age groups of 46-55; 56-65 and over 65. Likewise, FBSs within the younger age groups of 18-25; 26-35 and 36-45 are more likely to have problems family attachment and academic maladjustment issues than FBSs within the older age groups of 46-55; 56-65 and over 65.

Foreign-born students' marital status was not statistically significant in their PDCI and FAAM experience based on their responses to items on subscales B and C. ICHN was the only component (subscale A) where psycho-cultural adjustment was influenced by marital status. Therefore, when it comes to FBSs' adjustment to identity consciousness and home nostalgia (ICHN), it makes a statistically significant difference if a student was married, single or divorced. In relation to scale A, a post hoc test (Tukey HSD) indicated that FBSs who are divorced and single are more likely to experience psychological disorientation challenges as well as have potentials towards culturally inflexibility more than married FBSs.

Foreign-born students' continent of origin was not statistically significant in their ICHN and PDCI experience based on their responses to items on subscales A and B. FAAM was the only component (subscale C) where psycho-cultural adjustment was impacted by continent of origin.

Therefore, in adjustment to family attachment and academic maladjustment (FAAM) issues, it makes a statistically significant difference if you are from Asia, Africa, Latin America, Europe, North America, South America, or Middle East. In relation to scale C, a post hoc test (Tukey HSD) showed that FBSs from North America, the Middle East, Africa, and Asia are more likely to have family attachment and academic maladjustment challenges than FBSs from Europe, and Latin America.

Foreign-born students' year in college was not statistically significant in their PDCI and FAAM experience based on their responses to items on subscales B and C. ICHN was the only area of adjustment that was significantly influenced by FBSs year in college. So, in FBSs; adjustment to identity consciousness and home nostalgia (ICHN), it makes a statistically significant difference if the student was in year one, two or above year two at the CC. In relation to scale B, a post hoc test (Tukey HSD) showed that FBSs in year one are more likely to be impacted by psychological disorientation difficulties as well as have issues with cultural inflexibility than those in year two and above year two at CCs

Foreign-born students' family presence was not statistically significant in their ICHN and FAAM experiences based on their responses to items on subscales A and C. However, family presence influenced their adjustment to PDCI. Therefore, in FBSs' adjustment psychological disorientation and cultural inflexibility issues, it makes a statistically significant difference if the student has family here in the US or not. In relation to scale B, the associated descriptive statistics indicated that FBSs (the No group) who do not have their families present in the US are more likely to have identity consciousness and home nostalgia issues than FBSs (the yes group) with their families present in the US.

Based on the result of this survey, it could be empirically assumed that the post-migration psycho-cultural adjustment challenges of FBSs enrolled in CCs in the US relatively differ in statistical significance among groups, to a certain degree, based on age, year in college, continent of origin, marital status and family presence, with only gender excluded.

Research Question 3: To what extent and in what ways are post-migration psycho-cultural adjustment challenges related to the outcomes (social interaction and academic/career engagement) of foreign-born students' adjustment at CCs in the US?

This subsidiary research question was measured by items on Tables 18 and 19. This question was best answered by referring to the research and data analysis from the responses to the eleven items that address this query. The survey part of this study found that FBSs enrolled in CCs in the US are relatively well adjusted when it comes to social interaction, academic and career engagement. An inspection of the survey results, based on the frequency table associated with FBSs' level of opinions, general satisfaction with their CCs and career engagement, indicates the following:

FBSs' overwhelmingly responded in the affirmative (yes) to the following outcome-related items: plans to continue studies; plans to enroll in a four year college upon completion; satisfaction with life at the CC; desire to select CC again as a place of study; willingness to recommend the US to others for study on Table 18. These items on Table 18 have a cumulative mean for positive item response (yes) of 61.67% from IS participants and a cumulative mean for negative item response (no) of 21.13%; while 17.20% remained neutral (do not know). This means that, discounting negative and neutral IS respondents, approximately 62% of all FBSs' participants plan to continue studies; plan to enroll in a four year college upon completion; satisfied with life at the CC; desire to select CC again as a place of study; and willing to recommend the US to others for study. To the following items: "plans to return home after studies and feeling like dropping out of the CC," on Table 18, 45% of international participants indicated no; 34% indicated yes while 21% indicated do not know (neutral).

FBS responses to the following items: "feeling able to relate with Americans; prefer to relate only with my own people and have difficulty interacting with teachers here because of previous home experiences" help to determine the level of FBSs' social relationship and interaction in general. Table 19 showed a cumulative mean item disagreement of 49.47% and a cumulative mean item agreement of 25.97%; while 24.56% were undecided. This means that approximately 50% of FBSs signified disagreement or strong disagreement to the items on Table 19; approximately 26% of FBSs agreed to items on Table 19; while about 25% average of FBSs remained neutral.

Foreign-born students' responses to the outcome items on Tables 18 & 19 were used to determine as well as reveal the degree of impact psycho-cultural adjustment challenges may have left on FBSs at community colleges. Researcher believes that dispositions, experiences, expectations, thoughts and feelings of FBSs; based on the trend and degree of their psycho-cultural adjustment, might play a vital role in their social, academic, career decision-making and individual determinations. FBSs' general responses to items on Tables 18 and 19 indicated that their seemingly well-adjusted dispositions showed up, to a certain degree, in the frequency of their affirmative responses to specific items. These items were designed to suggest progress in FBSs' psycho-cultural adjustment as well as negative responses to items that denote FBSs' psycho-cultural maladjustment at their various CCs in the US.

General Conclusions

Preliminary survey and subsequent focus group interview findings point to potentially significant but lightly pronounced psycho-cultural adjustment challenges among foreign-born students at community colleges. While other cultural and cognitive theories could offer some explanations for these findings, this researcher recognizes that this mixed method research which utilized Likert-type subscale surveys and focus-group interview session was only explanatory in nature and the need for further study might be required.

Data from this research are certain to contribute to any future debate or literature on the psycho-cultural adjustment challenges of foreign-born students at community colleges. Nevertheless, a most reliable and definitive conclusion cannot be immediately drawn from this mixed method study at this time. However, there is sufficient evidence from statistical data and focus group interview results to confirm that FBSs at CCs in the US, indeed, face some degree of post-migration psycho-cultural adjustments challenges.

When a conclusion is drawn from only the survey study perspective, frequency of foreign-born students' responses and statistical data, based on a Likert-type subscale findings in this study; discounting possible statistical implications of FBSs' neutral responses, indications abound from available empirical data that FBSs at community colleges in the US face a low to no post-migration psycho-cultural adjustment challenges. It is assumed that because the mean level of interest was set by this researcher at 3.0., two subscales (A & B) of three (A, B &C) that stand for psycho-cultural adjustment construct did not equal nor exceed the 3.0 required midpoint making them low subscales of construct support. Moreover, of 34 items denoting FBSs' psycho-cultural tendencies; across the three subscales (subscales A, B & C), only 12 captured higher percentage means of FBSs' item agreement. Also, the cumulative mean agreement to all the items on the three subscales is 31.4% (below 50%). But there could have been some unmeasured variance based on certain statistical variables to permit a definitive conclusion at this point.

Overall, based on the quantitative data from the survey part of this study and the qualitative data gleaned from the focus group discussions, it could be reasonably assumed that FBSs at CCs in the US, to some extent, face a comparatively moderate to high level of post-migration psycho-cultural adjustment challenges. This research, therefore, expands the body of literature on the dissertation topic. It offers useful information and recommendations to be considered by researcher, policy-makers, administrators, IS advisors and counselors with tremendous implications for research, policy and practice.

Implications of the Findings

Based on the general review of literature and the mixed method research findings from this research, further discussions on findings would, to some extent, implicate identity consciousness and home nostalgia; psychological disorientation and cultural inflexibility; family attachment and academic maladjustment as potential correlates of psycho-cultural adjustment challenges among foreign-born students at community colleges. If directors of foreign-born students' services or administrators are concerned about FBSs' post-migration psycho-cultural adjustment challenges in their colleges and institutions, steps to mitigate FBSs' psycho-cultural adjustment challenges should be taken. A relatively good number of international student respondents claimed to be potentially influenced by the above mentioned compound psycho-cultural maladjustment components.

Research underscores some of the issues related to psycho-cultural adjustment challenges of foreign-born students at community colleges. Findings from this investigation have several implications for educational administration, policy and research. Based on findings, the following suggestions have been advanced for the improvement of FBSs' psycho-cultural adjustments at CCs. To mitigate these adjustment problems, the following implications and recommendations should be given priority of attention:

Recommendations for Community Colleges

The idea of reaching out, attracting, recruiting and retaining FBSs from various countries across the globe is of paramount importance. In order to satisfactorily accomplish these four essential missions and objectives, the provision and increase in the frequency and quality of psycho-cultural adjustment services to foreign-born students at community colleges is greatly recommended. CCs could provide outreach centers for FBSs in the United States to help reduce their apprehension about psycho-cultural adjustment as well as to foster a sense of belonging that will clear grounds for a more positive experience in the US. A cultural diversity training forums, workshops and seminars should also be introduced to encourage the provision of education on the psycho-cultural adjustment challenges of FBSs to their American counterparts. These provisions will lay strong emphasis on the recommendations that

Americans, despite their culturally individualistic and legalistic tendencies, should reach out more to their foreign-born (international) guests whose cultural-identity tendencies are more collectivistic and relationship oriented. By so doing, the gap that exists among people of different cultures coexisting in a given cultural environment can be more tolerably bridged.

Recommendations for Educators

Flexible application of best theories and practices will facilitate academic adjustment for foreign-born students at community colleges and at other institutions of higher learning. CCs and universities should develop appropriate education policies to improve FBSs' psycho-cultural academic adjustments. These education policies will entail hiring and training more staff to understand FBSs' pattern of thinking, feeling and response to a new cultural environment. This approach will enhance the level of FBSs' participation in essential class works and salient academic discussions giving their various idiosyncratic cultural backgrounds. This idea finds strong corroboration in Museus and Quaye's (2009) suggestion that if educators invest energy and resources in structuring opportunities to establish connections between new minority students and cultural agents, those educators might maximize their impact if those opportunities emphasize both educational goals and validate FBSs' cultural heritages.

Recommendations for Policy Makers

The prospects of attracting and retaining foreign-born students at community colleges and higher institutions of learning, develop policies and intervention strategies to improve their overall enrollment should be of absolute importance to policy makers. In this vein, policy makers should introduce programs at colleges and universities that encourage understanding of the psycho-cultural background and challenges of FBSs if they wish to effectively serve those special groups of students. In a generation when programs are being restructured to recruit more FBSs into higher institutions of learning in the United States, the need to consider the potentially positive impact of mandatory FBSs' affinity groups and organizations is crucial. Empirical data could even be utilized by policy makers in advocating ways these FBS groups and organizations promote the well-being of FBSs. Policy makers should also ensure that sufficient support to help such FBS groups and organizations flourish exists on their common agendas for improvement in the student's lives at colleges and universities. Policies that encourage federal government's support on FBSs ought to recommend salient resources to help FBSs experience a positive social life. Networks with both FBSs and their American counterparts need to be incorporated into strategic international psycho-cultural education policy decisions.

Recommendations for Administrators

Findings from data analyses and the emergent psycho-cultural perspectives have several proximate implications for administrators. On staff recruitment process, findings underscore that insufficient hiring and training of IS affairs staff and counselors might impede potential understanding as well as decrease valuable insights into these *core* challenges in FBSs' adjustment. In the context of adjustment, administrators should note that the powerful and pervasive nature of FBSs' psycho-cultural well-being could influence their entire life on campus yet psycho-cultural perspectives are rarely employed in assessing and evaluating FBSs. It appears that the knowledge of the psycho-cultural concept may constitute a useful tool in conceptualizing the administrative decision-making during the hiring process of the FBSs' affairs directors, staff and counselors. As CCs and universities experience various structural diversifications, administrators should consider how campus climate could possibly enhance the experiences of this special class of students from increasingly diverse cultural backgrounds across the globe. Administrators could do this by exposing FBSs, from the onset, to various psycho-cultural environments and social systems to which these minority students are expected to become adjusted and acclimatized. This is consistent with Kuh and Love's (2000) contention that administrators and staff should seek to make the strange seem familiar early in students' college experiences. Therefore, clarion calls from administrators regarding the importance of studying deep aspects of other people's culture and their role in streamlining the experiences of FBSs at colleges and universities should be sufficiently encouraged.

Recommendations for Counselors

Since the provision of counseling services on the community college campuses for foreign-born students ought to strongly incorporate the hiring and training of counselors and mental health practitioners, FBSs' counselors should be ready to receive special trainings to enable them enhance their proficiency in offering psycho-culturally sensitive services to FBSs. Improper identification and diagnosis of psycho-cultural stressors by incompetent counselors may result in both overlooking major psycho-cultural challenges and attributing life crisis resulting from sorely missed cultural values, ideologies, attitudes, convictions and philosophical assumptions to mental sickness. Counselors should strive to understand the root causes of FBSs' maladjustment behaviors to enable them clarify roles and expectations effectively to their FBS (international student) clients. In order to accomplish this objective, efforts should be creatively made by counselors and caseworkers to understand the complexity, intensity, sensitivity and prevalence of the psycho-cultural adjustment challenges that FBSs face for better counseling interventions.

Future Research Directions

Findings from this research have implications for future research. First, subsequent research is needed to determine whether the apparent fundamental subscales; underpinning foreign-born students' post-migration psycho-cultural maladjustment and the consequent challenges, are representative of the feelings, beliefs, and experiences of FBSs in other geographical areas, regions and environment in the US. Future research is needed to further explore an in-depth qualitative psycho-cultural domains, components and characteristics identified in this present study. This level of research might be better conducted on a wider scale because this particular study provides only a panorama of subscales that predict psycho-cultural adjustment difficulties among FBSs at community colleges in the northeastern US. Researchers may wish to replicate and expand this study with a more focused approach on developing more intimate researcher and participant relationships. Namely, it might be more productive to engage participants in one-on-one discussions, for a more profound dialogue on the subscales that predict psycho-cultural adjustment challenges among FBSs on a foreign soil. This type of prospective subtle change in methodology might simplify the process of identifying and categorizing data as well as make study more qualitative. It will enable the investigator to ask more probing questions as well as collect information in a more intimate and expressive level. In particular, additional information about phenomena will be gathered if participants are granted enough latitude and privacy to respond to interview questions.

As suggested by this research and by previous research related to integrated psychological and cultural adjustment of foreign-born students, if the psycho-cultural correlates of FBSs' adjustment typically varied across FBSs from different continents, then future studies will necessarily rest upon a consideration, assumption and incorporation of these differences in a more conspicuous fashion. Setting up an improved research design might include hypothesis testing and more detailed data analyses. It would be of value if a similar sample from different geographical regions or higher institutions of learning are tested using a similar instrument. Since research was done only in the community college setting, future research could examine post-migration psycho-cultural adjustment challenges in other contexts such as in high schools as well as in four year colleges and universities.

Also, since study is a learning experience, it might be helpful to make survey more open ended so as to dig deeper for a more significant data that are heavily qualitative oriented. This will give room for non-participants in the focus group interview sessions to represent their thoughts more profoundly. A more elaborate future study may, as well, use a *longitudinal* survey research approach with a view to tracking possible improvements or relapses in adjustment overtime. Future research would certainly benefit from investigating this phenomenon in greater details.

Actual Limitations of the Present Study

A number of limitations must be noted in considering the results of this study. The major limitation to this study was that cooperation from a few participating community colleges was to some degree limited and restrictive. Various frustrating strategies and delay tactics were adopted by some college representatives and designated contact persons. Attempts to get around signified non-cooperation and other difficulties posed by one of the participating CCs were enormously harrowing, at worst, for this researcher. In some cases, differences in what was supposed to have been a welcoming atmosphere were very frustrating. As a result, data collection was made within the constraints permitted by each participating CC. Participants for the focus-group session were more easily tracked and recruited through local libraries and communities. Some of the colleges signified their unwillingness and readiness to cooperate fully with this researcher as regards survey data collection only at the eleventh hour. Therefore, future studies of this nature might be better conducted when sponsored by the government (state or national level) or done by an institution itself. Nonetheless, responses from the focus group participants strongly supported and complemented the data needed for this study.

The fact that this researcher examined only three community colleges in the Northeastern US is a major limitation. Research is therefore not able to generalize these findings to other CCs and other kinds of undergraduate colleges and universities. Because of the perceived difficulty to glean more relevant psycho-cultural information as well as collect useful data from a wide variety of cultural respondents through typical needs assessment, data gathering methods such as face to face (one-on-one) discussions, and even on-site observations, the survey technique and focus group discussions, were rather preferred. To better address this challenge, future research could also utilize multiple research designs as well as methodologies like qualitative method that involves one-on-one discussions, ethnographic, quasi-experimental, or experimental designs if applicable.

Further limitations include threat to trustworthiness, credibility, and respondent's biases since I provided the survey to college representatives who in turn distributed the surveys to foreign-born students via the FBS coordinators on behalf of this researcher. In the presumed presence of a class instructor or administrative personnel, an FBS respondent might write or say what he or she thinks the researcher wants to see and perhaps paint only positive pictures of situations that are not altogether positive. Preservation of FBSs' and institutional anonymity and unanticipated restrictions to study by some community colleges, for various reasons, did prevent the possibility of sorting the samples based on certain demographic information. Instead all surveys were analyzed collectively and categorized based on the nature of each sample and limited information made available to researcher. Completion of data may have been incomplete or selective as a result. The same might be applicable to a focus group scenario where peers from the same college, country or continent are present as co-discussants. This could have some effects on the collection and analysis of empirical evidence. However, in this study, efforts were strategically made by this researcher to reduce such biases and its effects on the collection and analyses of empirical evidence.

Concluding Remarks

This research project sought to examine the psycho-cultural adjustment challenges of foreign-born students at community colleges in the Northeastern United States. This study utilized an explanatory mixed method design (Creswell, 2002). The design involved the use of a survey instrument and focus group discussions. As the researcher I collected quantitative and qualitative data in two phases from available participants at three CCs in Northeastern United States: 1). collecting quantitative data and 2). collecting qualitative data later to help explain the quantitative data results. Both the quantitative and qualitative data collection instruments (survey questionnaire and focus-group guide questions) were structured in such a way as to present a general picture of the research problem. The collection of qualitative data through a focus-group session was needed to explain, extend, and refine the result of the survey data collected. This approach enabled this researcher to address the research questions and three other subsidiary questions posed. The data collected were analyzed using descriptive and inferential statistics.

It is clear from this research on the foreign-born students' psycho-cultural adjustment challenges at community colleges that specific areas need to be improved upon with a view to ensuring that FBSs are provided with sufficiently appropriate services. These services will help ease their adjustment challenges as well as facilitate a more positive adjustment process. Concerted efforts to improve upon services provided to FBSs in this direction will enable CCs and other higher institutions of learning in the United States and elsewhere to better reach out, attract, recruit, and retain more FBSs in this competitive age of globalization.

References

Adler, P. (2002). Beyond cultural identity: Reflections and multiculturalism. Retrieved February 6, 2010 from http://www.mediate.com/articles/adler3.cfm.

Altbach, P. G. & Teichler, U. (2001). Internationalization and exchanges in a globalized university. *Journal of Studies in International Education, 5,* 5 –25.

Altbach, P.G. (2004). Globalization and the university: Myths and realities in an unequal world. *Tertiary Education and Management, 10 (1),* 3 –25.

Altbach, P. G. (2004). Higher education crosses borders: Can the United States remain the top destination for foreign students? *Change.* 36 (2) 18 –24.

American association of community colleges*: Research and statistics.* January, 2012.

Anbari, F.T., Khilkhanova, E., Romanova, M., & Umpleby, S. (2004). Managing cultural differences in international projects. *Journal of International Business and Economics, 2(1),* 267-274.

Arum, S., & van de Water, J. (1992). The need for a definition of international education in US universities. In C. Klasek (Ed.), *Bridges to the future: Strategies for internationalizing higher education* (pp. 191 –203). Carbondale, IL: Association of International Education Administrators.

Bahvala, A. (2002). Common stressors for international students in the USA. Retrieved February 14, 2009, from the Alumni Internet Access and Training Program website: http://alumni.iatp.org.ua/publications.

Bain, O. & Cummings, W. K. (2005). Where have the international students gone? *International Educator, 14(2),* 18 –26.

Belozersky, I. (1990). New beginnings, old problems. Psycho-cultural frame of reference and family dynamics during the adjustment period. *Journal of Jewish Communal Service.* 67:2, January 1990.

Benhabib, S. (1999). The liberal imagination and the four dogmas of multiculturalism. *The Yale Journal of Criticism, 12 (2),* 401–413.

Barletta, J. & Kobayashi, Y. (2007). Cross-cultural counseling with internationals students *Australian Journal of Guidance and Counseling, 17, (2),* 182 –194

Berger, K. S (2001). *The developing person through the life span* (5th ed.) New York: NY, Von Hoffman Press, Inc.

Berkner, L., He, S., Lew, S., Cominole, M., Siegel, P., & Griffith, J. (2005). *2003-2004 National postsecondary student aid study (NPSAS: 04): Student financial aid estimates for 2003-2004.* Washington, DC: U.S. Department of Education, National Center for Education Statistics.

Blair-Broeker, C.T., & Ernst, R.M. (2003). *Thinking About Psychology.* New York: Worth.

Borjas G. J. (2002). Rethinking foreign students. *National Review,* 17 June.

Breger, L. (2009). *From instinct to identity: The development of personality,* Hillsdale, NJ: Analytic Press.

Brehm, S. S., Kassim, S. M. & Fein, S. (2002). *Social Psychology* (5th ed). Boston, MA; Houghton Mifflin Company.

Brettel, C.B., &Hollifield, J.F. (2000). Migration theory. Talking across discipline. London, UK: Routledge.

Brewer, A.K. (2005). International student adjustment, technology use and English language learning in academia. PhD dissertation, The American University, Washington, DC: (UMI No. AAT 3164805).

Brickman, B., & Nuzzo, R. (1999). *International versus immigrant ESL students: Designing curriculum and programs to meet the needs of both.* Las Vegas: Community College of Southern Nevada, Department of International Languages. (ERIC Document Reproduction Services No. ED 426 610).

Brilliant, J. (2000) Issues in counseling immigrant college students. *Community College Journal of Research and Practice*, 24: 577 – 586

Bryman, A. (2006). Integrating quantitative and qualitative research: How is it done? Qualitative Research, 6, (1), 97 –114.

Burrell, K. I., & Kim, K. J. (2002). International students and academic assistance: Meeting the needs of another college population. In P. L. Dwinell & J. L. Higbee (Eds.), *Developmental education: Meeting diverse student needs*. Morrow, GA: National Association for Developmental Education

Bystritsky, A. (2006). Treatment-resistant anxiety disorders, *Molecular Psychiatry, 11(9),* 805–14.

Calleja, D. (2000). The world at your door. *Canadian Business, 73(20),* 108 –111.

Carnevale, A. P. (1999). Diversity in higher education: Why corporate America cares. *Diversity Digest.* Washington, DC: Association of American Colleges and Universities.

Chavajay, P., & Skowronek, J. (2008). Aspects of acculturation stress among international students attending a university in the USA. *Psychological Reports*, 103(3), 827-835. Doi:10.2466/PRO.103.3.827-835.

Charmaz, C. (2000) Grounded theory: Objectivist and constructivist methods. In N. Denzin & Y. Lincoln (Eds.) *Handbook of Qualitative Research.* 2nd ed. London, UK: Sage.

Chen, C. P. (1999). Common stressors among international college students: Research and counseling implications. *Journal of College Counseling, 2(1),* 49–65.

Chen. P. (2003). Factors influencing academic success of Chinese international students in Los Angeles community colleges. EdD dissertation, University of Southern California, United States-California. (UMI No.AAT 3133248).

Chen, D. (2008). International education at American community colleges. *Community College Enterprise, 14 (1).*

Cheng, H. C. (2004). Being ill in a foreign land: international students' perceptions of and experiences with university health services. *Kaleidoscope: A Graduate Journal of Qualitative Communication Research, 3,* 70–92.

Conover, P.J. (2009). Citizens Identities and Conceptions of the Self. *Journal of Political Philosophy, 3 (2),* pp. 133-165.

Ciguralova, D. K. (2005). Psychosocial adjustment of international students. *ColoradoState University Journal of Student Affairs, 14,* 17–24.

Cohen, M. C. (2007). Responding to the barriers to academic success for local international students as an avenue to student success and to the internationalization of a community college. Dissertation, George Mason University, United States-Virginia. (UMI No. AAT 3252965).

Clark, B. R. (1960). *The open door college*. New York, NY: McGraw-Hill.

Colorado State University (1993). *Colorado State University tutorial on validation* Retrieved on July 26, 2010 fromhttp://writing.colostate. edu/guides/ research/ relval/index.cfm Community College Times (2009). Two-year colleges lead in international student growth Retrieved December20, 2009 from http://www.community collegetimes.com/topic.cfm? Topcld-58.

Conover, P.J. (2009). Citizens identities and conceptions of the self. *Journal of Political Philosophy, 3 (2),* 133 –165.

Constantine, M. G., Kindaichi, M., Okazaki, S., Gainor, K. A., & Baden, A. L. (2005). A qualitative investigation of the cultural adjustment experiences of Asian international college women. *Cultural Diversity and Ethnic Minority Psychology, 11 (2),* 162–175

Cox, R. D. (2009). *The college fear factor: How students and professors misunderstood one another.* Cambridge, Massachusetts: Harvard University Press.

Crawford, J. (2000). *At war with diversity: US language policy in an age of anxiety*. New York, NY: Multilingual Matters.

Creswell, J. W. (2002). *Educational research: Planning, conducting and evaluation qualitative and quantitative research.* Upper Saddle River, NJ: Pearson Education, Inc.

Creswell, J. W. (2003). Research *design: Qualitative, quantitative, and mixed methods approaches (2nd ed.).* Thousand Oaks, CA: Sage Publications.

Creswell, J. W & Miller, D. L. (2000). Determining validity in qualitative inquiry. *Theory into Practice, 39(3),* 124-131.

Creswell, J. W., & Plano-Clark, V. L. (2007). *Designing and conducting mixed methods research.* Thousand Oaks, CA: Sage Inc.

Curlette, W. L. (2006). A framework for research studies: Mixed methods through combining Bayesian statistics and qualitative research in individual psychology. *The Journal of Individual Psychology, 62(3),* 2006, 338-349

Davis, T. (Ed.) (1998). Open *doors: 1997/98 report on international educational exchange.* New York, NY: Institute of International Education.

Dia, I. A. (2005). Migrations internationals estudiantes, internationalization del'enseignement suprrieur et fuite des cerveaux. *Global Perspectives, 54.* Available at http://www.unhcr.org/ refworld/docid/43a2ced14.html[Accessed17 May 2010].

Doku, N. S. (2007). International student experiences at two Midwestern community colleges: Voices from within. EdD dissertation, University of Kansas. Lawrence, KS. (UMI No. AAT 3274492).

Dwindell, P. L., & Higbee, J. L. (Eds.). (1998) *Developmental education: Meeting diverse student needs.* Morrow, GA: National Association for Development Education.

Erikson, E. H. (1968). *Identity, youth and crisis*. New York, NY: Norton

Erskine, T. (2002). "Citizen of nowhere" or "the point where circles intersect?" Impartialist and embedded cosmopolitanism.' *Review of International Studies, 28 (3),* 457-478.

Florida, R., (2005). *The flight of the creative class: The new global competition for talent.* New York, NY: Harper Collins.

Fritz, M. V., Chin, D., & DeMarinis, V. (2008). Stressors, anxiety, acculturation and adjustment among international and North American students. *International Journal of Intercultural Relations, 32(3),* 244-259. doi:10.1016/j.ijintrel.2008.01.001

Frost, M. (2002). *Constituting human rights: Global civil society and the society of democratic and democratizing states.* London: Routledge.

Gay, L. R., & Airasian, P. (2003). *Educational research: Competencies for analysis and application* (7th ed.). Upper Saddle River, NJ: Pearson Education.

Geiger, R.L. (1986). *Private Sectors in Higher Education: Structure, Function and Change in Eight Countries.* Ann Arbor: University of Michigan Press.

George, D., & Mallery, P. (2003). SPSS for windows step by step: A simple guide and reference 11.0 update. (4th ed.). Boston, MA: Allyn and Bacon.

Giangreco, M. F. (2010). One-to-one paraprofessionals for students with disabilities in inclusive classrooms: Is conventional wisdom wrong? *Intellectual & Developmental Disabilities, 48(1),* 1–13. doi: 10.1352/1934-9556-48.1.1

Gloria, A. M., & Ho, T. A (2003). Environmental, social and psychological experiences of Asian American undergraduates: Examining Issues of academic persistence. *Journal of Counseling and Development, 81(1),* 93 –105.

Gregory, S. (1997). Planning for the increase in foreign-born students. *Planning for Higher Education, 26,* 23 –28.

Grusky S., (2000). International service learning. *American Behavioral Scientist, 43, (5),* 858 –86.

Gudykunst, W. & Kim, Y. Y. (1997).*Communicating with strangers: An approach to intercultural communication* (3rd ed.). New York, NY: McGraw-Hill, Inc.

Harari, M. (1992).*The internationalization of the curriculum.* In C.B. Klasek (Ed.), *Bridges to the future: Strategies for internationalizing higher education* pp.52-79. Carbondale, IL: Association of International Education Administrators.

Harper S. R., & Quaye, S. J. (Eds) (2009) *Student engagement in higher education: Theoretical perspectives and practical approaches for diverse populations.* New York, NY: Taylor and Francis Group.

Hartshorne, R., & Baucom, J. (2007). Issues affecting cross-cultural adaptation of international students. *Multicultural Learning and Training, 2 (2),* 78–87.

Hatch, J.A. (2002). Doing qualitative research in education settings. Albany, NY: State University of New York Press

Hazen, H.C & Alberts, H.C. (2006).Visitors or immigrants? International students in the United States population. *Space Place 12,* 201–216.

Hechanova-Alampay, R., Beehr, T.A., Christiansen, N. D. & Van Horn, R K (2002). Adjustment and strain among domestic and international student sojourners: A longitudinal study. *School Psychology International 23 (4),* 458–74.

Heine, S. J., Kitayama S., Lehman, D. R., Takata, T., Matsumoto, H., Ide, E. & Leung, C. (2001). Divergent consequences of success and failure in Japan and North America: An investigation of self-improving motivations and malleable selves. *Journal of Personality and Social Psychology, 81 (4),* 599–615.

Hofstede, G. (2000). *Culture's consequences: comparing values, behaviors, institutions, and organization across nations.* 2nd edition. Thousand Oaks: Sage Publications.

Hofstede, G., Hofstede, G. J. & Minkov, M. (2010). *Cultures and Organizations: Software of the Mind* (Rev. 3rd ed.). New York: McGraw-Hill.

Hogg, M. A., & Williams, D. F. (2000). From I to we: Social identity and the collective self. *Groups Dynamics: Theory, Research, and Practice, 4 (1),* 81-97.

Hurtado, S., Milem, J. F., Clayton-Pedersen, A., & Allen.W. R. (1998). Enhancing campus climates for racial/ethnic diversity: Educational policy and practice. *The Review of Higher Education, 21(3),* 279–302.

Hughes, H. (2004). Researching the experience of international students In P. A. Danaher, C. Macpherson, F. Nouwens, & D. Orr (Eds.), *Lifelong learning: Whose responsibility and what is your contribution? Refereed papers from the 3rd International Lifelong Learning Conference*, Yeppoon, Australia. 13-16 June, (pp. 168-174). Rockhampton: Central Queensland University Press.

Hwang, M. H., & Heppner, M. J. (2001). *Korean career choices: Cross-cultural validity of measures and inventories.* Paper presented at the annual meeting of the American Psychological Association, San Francisco, CA.

Hyun, J., Quinn, B., Madon, T., & Lustig, S. (2007). Mental health need, awareness, and use of counseling services among international graduate students. Journal of American College Health, 56 (2), 109-118.

Institute of International Education (2011). Open Doors 200. Retrieved September 2, 2011 from http://www.opendoors.iienetwork.org/?=150649

International and the role of university networks (2009): *Proceedings of the Emuni conference of higher education and research*, Potoroz, Slovenia, 25–26 September.

Johnson, K. A. (1993). *Q-Methodology: Perceptions of international student services in Higher Education.* (ERIC Document Reproduction Service No. ED363550).

Kagitcibasi, C. (2005). Autonomy and relatedness in cultural context. *Journal of Cross Cultural Psychology, 36 (4),* 403–422.

Kaczmarek, P. G., Matlock, G., Merta, R., Ames, M.H., & Ross, M. (1994). An assessment of international college student adjustment. *International Journal for the Advancement of Counseling, 17*, 241–247.

Kalsner, L., & Pistole, C.M. (2003). College adjustment in a multiethnic sample: Attachment, separation-individuation, and ethnic identity. *Journal of College Student Development, 44*(1), 92-109.

Keller, G. (1983). *Academic Strategy. The management revolution in American higher education.* Baltimore, MD: Johns Hopkins University Press.

Khoo, P. L. S., Abu-Rasain, M. H., & Hornby, G. (2002). Counseling foreign students: A review of strategies. In S. Palmer (Ed.), *Multicultural counselling: A reader* pp. 98–113. London, UK: Sage Publications.

Kim, Y. Y. (2002). Cross-cultural adaptation: An integrative theory. In J. M. Martin, T. K. Nakayama, & L. A. Flores (Eds.), *Readings in cultural contexts* (2nd ed., pp 237-245). Mountain View, CA: Mayfield.

Kim, Y. Y., & Gudykunst, W. B. (1992). Communicating *with strangers*. New York, NY: McGraw-Hill.

Kim, B. S. K., & Omizo, M. M. (2003). Asian cultural values, attitudes toward seeking professional psychological help, and willingness to see a counselor. *The Counseling Psychologist, 31, 343-361.*

Kim, Y.U., Triandis, H.C., Kagitcibasi, C., Choi, S.C., & Yoon, G. (1994). Individualism and collectivism: Theory, method and applications. Thousand Oaks, CA: Sage.

King, R., & Ruiz-Gelices, E. (2003). International student migration and the European 'year abroad': Effects on European identity and subsequent migration behavior. *International Journal of Population Geography, 9*, 229–252.

Kisell, L. L. (2007). High hopes and current realities: Conceptual metaphors and meaning for English language learners at the community college. PhD dissertation, The University of Arizona, Tucson, AZ. (UMI No. AAT 3240018).

Komiya, N., & Eells, G. T. (2001, fall). Predictors of attitudes toward seeking counseling among international students. *Journal of College Counseling, 4 (2),* 153–171.

Kosic, A. (2002), Acculturation attitudes, need for cognitive closure, and adaptation of immigrants, *The Journal of Social Psychology, 142 (2),* 179–201.

Krathowohl, D. (2004). *Methods of educational & social science research: An integrated approach* (2nd ed.). New York, NY: Longman, Addison–Wesley.

Kroger, J. (2000). *Identity development: Adolescence through adulthood.* Thousand Oaks, CA: Sage Publications, Inc.

Krosteng, M.V. (1992). Predicting persistence from the student adaptation to college questionnaire: Early warning or siren song? Research in Higher Education, *33(1),* 99-111.

Krueger, R. A. (1994). *Focus groups*: A practical guide for applied research. (2nd Ed.). Newbury Park, CA: Sage

Krueger, R. A., & Casey, M. A. (2000). Focus groups: A practical guide for applied researchers (3rd ed.). Thousand Oaks, CA: Sage.

Kuh, G. D., & Love, P. G. (2000). A cultural perspective on student departure. In J. Braxton (Ed.), *Rethinking the departure puzzle: New theory and research on college student retention.* Nashville, TN: Vanderbilt University Press.

Lamkin, A. (2000). International *Students at Community Colleges*. CA: Los Angeles, Eric Clearing House.

Lawley, M. (1993). *Factors influencing the choice of destination in international university education: the case of Hong Kong student.* Unpublished masters thesis, University of Southern Queensland, Toowoomba.

Lee, J. & Rice, C. (2007). Welcome to America? International student perceptions of discrimination. *Higher Education, 53* (3), 381–409.

Leong, F. T. L., & Chou, E. L., (2002). Counseling international students and sojourners.

In P. B. Pedersen, J. G. Draguns, W. J. Lonner, & J. E. Trimble (Eds.). *Counseling across cultures* (5th ed.) pp. 185–207).

Leslow-Hurley, J. (2000). The foundations of dual language instruction. New program suggestions. *College Student Journal, 31,* 473–479.

Li, A. & Gasser, M. B. (2005). Predicting Asian international students' sociocultural adjustment: A test of two mediation models. *International Journal of Intercultural Relations, 29* (5), 561–576.

Lin, J. C., & Yi, J. K. (1997). Asian international students' adjustment: Issues and program suggestions. *College student Journal, 31,* 473 – 484.

Linklater, A. (2007). 'Distant suffering and cosmopolitan obligations,' *International Politics, 44,* 19-36.

Lumby, J. (2006).International perspectives on leadership and management. *Management in Education*, Vol. 20, No.4, pp.7-10.

Marginson, S. & Sawir, E. (2011). *Ideas for intercultural education.* New York, NY: Palgrave Macmillan.

Martin, J. N., Nakayama, T. K., & Flores, L. A. (2002) *Readings in intercultural communication: Experiences and contexts.* New York, NY: McGraw Hill.

Marx, E. (2001), *Breaking through culture shock: What you need to succeed in international business.* Boston, MA: Nicholas Brealey.

Mattanah, J.F., Hancock, G.R., & Brand, B.L. (2004). Parental attachment, separation individuation and college student adjustment: A structural equation analysis of mediational effects. *Journal of Counseling Psychology, 51(2),* 213 – 225.

Mazzarol, T, & Soutar, G. (2002). 'Push-Pull' factors influencing international students' destination choice. *The International Journal of Educational Management 16 (2)*, 82 – 90.

Mishal, S., & Morag, N. (2002) Political expectations and cultural perceptions in the Arab-Israeli peace negotiations. *Political Psychology, 23 (2),* 352-353.doi: 10.1111/0162-895X.00284

Misra, R., Crist, M., & Burant, C. J. (2003). Relationship among life stress, social support, academic stressors, and reactions to stressors of international students in the United States. *International Journal of Stress Management, 10,* 137–157.

Mori, S. (2000).Addressing the mental health concerns of international students. *Journal of Counseling and Development, 78(2),* 138–144.

Moshman, D. (2005) *Adolescent psychological development: Rationality, morality and identity* (2nded). New York, NY: Wiley.

Museus, S. D., & Quaye, S. J. (2009). Toward an intercultural perspective of racial and ethnic minority college student persistence. *Review of Higher Education, 33 (1),* 67–94.

Neuliep, J. W. (2006). *Intercultural communication: A contextual approach (3rd ed.).* Thousand Oaks, CA: Sage Publications.

Neuliep, J. W. (2008). *Intercultural Communication: A contextual approach (4th ed.).* Thousand Oaks, CA: Sage Publications.

Neuman, W. L., (2000). *Social research methods: Qualitative and quantitative approaches* (4th ed.). Boston, MA: Allyn and Bacon.

Nilsson, J. E., & Anderson, A. Z. (2004). Supervising international students: The role of acculturation, role ambiguity, and multicultural discussions. *Professional Psychology: Research and Practice, 35,* 306–312.

Nilsson, J. E., Berkel, L. A., Flores, L. Y., & Lucas, M. S. (2004). Utilization rate and presenting concerns of international students at a university counseling center: Implications for outreach programming. *Journal of College Student Psychotherapy. 19 (2),* 49–59.

Oberg, K. (1960). 'Culture shock': Adjustment to new cultural environments. *Practical Anthropology 7,* 177–82.

Open Doors. (2010). The *annual report of international education.* Institute of International Education. Retrieved fromhttp://opendoors.iienetwork.org

Open Doors. (2011). The *annual report of international education.* Institute of International Education. Retrieved from http://www.iie.org/opendoors.

Organization for Economic Cooperation and Development (2002). *Education at a Glance*: OECD indicators 2002 and 2004. Paris: Author.

Oyserman, D., Coon, H.M., & Kemmelmeier, M. (2002). Rethinking individualism and collectivism: Evaluation of theoretical assumptions and meta-analysis. *Psychological Bulletin, 128,* 3 – 72.

Patton, M. Q. (2002). Qualitative *research and methods evaluation (3rd ed.).* Thousand Oaks, CA: Sage.

Papastergiadis, N. (2000). *The turbulence of migration, deterritorialization and hybridity* Cambridge, MA: Polity Press.

Pedersen, T. B. (1991). Counseling international students. *Counseling Psychologist, 19,* 10–58.

Pedersen, P. (1995). *The five stages of culture shock: Critical incidents around the world.* Westport, CT: Sage Publications.

Pimpa, N. (2003). The influence of family on Thai students' choices of international education. *The International Journal of Educational Management, 17 (5),* 211–219.

Plotnik, R. (2002). *Introduction to Psychology*, 6th ed. Belmont, CA: Wadsworth – Thomson Learning.

Portes, P. & Madelon, F. (2001). *Differential predictors of mathematics and reading achievement: What may be learned from immigrant adolescents' adaptation to school.* Paper presented at the Annual Meeting of the American Educational Research Association, Seattle, WA. Russell Sage and Spencer Foundations.

Poyrazli, S., Arbona, C., Nora, A., McPherson, R., & Pisecco, S. (2002). Relation between assertiveness, academic self-efficacy, and psychosocial adjustment among international graduate students. *Journal of College Student Development, 43 (5),* 632–643.

Quatroche, D. J. (2000). Helping the underachiever in reading. *ERIC Review, 7, 25–26.* Rajapaksa, S. & Dundes, L. S. L (2003). 'It's a long way home:' International student adjustment to living in the United States. *College Student Retention. 4 (1),* 15–28.

Rizvi, F. (2005). *International education and the production of cosmopolitan identities.* Paper presented at the Transnational Seminar Series (March 4), Urbana-Champaign, IL.

Robertson, M., Line, M., Jones, S., & Thomas, S. (2000). International students, learning environments and perceptions: A case study using the Delphi technique. *Higher Education Research & Development, 19 (1),* 89–102.

Ross, M. H, (2001). Psychocultural interpretation and dramas: Identity dynamics in ethnic conflict. *Political Psychology, 22 (1), 157-178,* doi: 10.1111/0162-895X. 00231

Rubin, A., & Babbie, E. (2001). Research *methods in social work research: Challenges and rewards.* Thousand Oaks, CA: Sage.

Ryan, M. E., & Twibell, R. S. (2000). Concerns, values, stress, coping, health and educational outcomes of college students who studies abroad. *International Journal of Intercultural Relations, 24,* 409–435.

Sadeghi, M., Fischer, J. M., & House, S. G. (2003). Ethical dilemmas in multicultural counseling. *Journal of Multicultural Counseling and Development, 31 (3),* 179–192.

Sakurako, M. (2000). Addressing the mental health concerns of international students. *Journal of Counseling and Development, 78(2),* 137–144.

Sam, D. L. (2001). Satisfaction with life among international students: An exploratory study. *Social Indicators Research, 53, 315-322.*

Samovar, L. A., Porter, R. E. & Stephani, L. A. (2000). Communication between cultures (3rd ed). Beijing: Foreign Language Teaching and Research Press

Schmitt, M. T., Spears, R., & Branscombe, N. R. (2003). Constructing a minority group identity out of shared rejection: The case of international students. *European Journal of Social Psychology, 33,* 1–12.

Schramm-Nielsen, J. (2002) *Conflict management in Scandinavia. JACM 15te Annual Conference.* Retrieved on February 18, 2010 from http://papers.ssm.com/ so13/ papers.cfm? abstract_id=305153

Schuster, J., & Finkelstein, M. J. (2006). *The restructuring of academic work and careers: The American faculty.* Baltimore, MA: Johns Hopkins University Press.

Selmer, J. (1999). Effects of coping strategies on sociocultural and psychological adjustment of western expatriate managers in the PRC. *Journal of World Business, 34(1),* 41–51.

Selmer, J. (2002). Practice makes perfect? International experience and expatriate adjustment. *Management International Review, 42(1),* 71–87.

Selvadurai, R. (1998). Problems faced by international students in American colleges and universities. *Community Review, 16,* 153–158.

Sheldon, P. (2009). Being ill in a foreign country: International students' trust in American physicians. *Journal of Intercultural Communication, 19.* Available online: http://www.immi.se/intercultural/nr19/pavica.htm

Singelis, T. M. (2000). Some thoughts on the future of cross-cultural social psychology. *Journal of Cross-Cultural Psychology, 31 (1),* 76–91.

Smith, M. S. (1986). The whole is greater: Combining qualitative and quantitative approaches in evaluation studies. In D. D. Williams (Ed). *Naturalistic evaluation: New directions for program evaluation, 30.* (pp. 37–54). San Francisco, CA: Jossey-Bass.

Spellings, M. (2005). EjournalUSA, http://usinfo.state.gov/journals/itsv/1105/ijse/spellings.htm.

Spencer-Rodgers, J., & McGovern, T. (2002). Attitudes towards the culturally different: The role of intercultural communication barriers, affective responses, consensual stereotypes and perceived threat. *International Journal of Intercultural Relations, 26 (6),* 609–631.

Stabb, S. D., Harris, S.M., & Talley, J. S. (1995) *Multicultural needs assessment for college and university student populations,* Springfield: IL Charles C. Thomas Publisher.

Steinberg, L. D., & Morris, A. S. (2001). Annual *review of psychology, 52*: 83–110.

Strauss, A. L., & Corbin, J. (1998). Basics of qualitative research: Techniques and procedures for developing grounded theory (2nd ed.). Newbury Park, CA: Sage.

Stroman, J. S. D., (2004). Case study of a college ESL program. Ph.D. dissertation, The University of Texas at Austin, Texas. (UMI No. AAT 3145803).

Stronquist, N. P., &Monkman, K. (Eds) (2000*). Globalization and education: Integration and contestation across cultures.* Lanham, MD: Rowman & Littlefield.

Suárez-Orozco, C., Suárez-Ororzco, M. M., & Todorova, I. (2008). Learning *in a new land: Immigrant students in American society.* Cambridge, MA: The Belknap Press of Harvard University Press.

Sumer, S., Poyrazli, S. & Grahame, K. (2008). Predictors of depression and anxiety among international students. *Journal of Counseling and Development. 86 (4)*, 429–437.

Swami, V., Arteche, A., Chamorro-Premuzic, T., & Furnham, A. (2009). Sociocultural adjustment among sojourning Malaysian students in Britain: A replication and path analytic extension. *Social Psychiatry and Psychiatric Epidemiology*, Retrieved on October 29, 2011 from http://www. springerlink.com / content/d1785772u1663580/fulltext.pdf.

Swagler, M. & Ellis, M. (2003). The Adaptation of Taiwanese graduate students in the US: Impact of language ability, communication apprehension, social contact, and cultural differences. *Journal of Counseling Psychology, 51*, 420-437.

Tatar, M., & Horenczyk, G. (2000). Counseling students on the move: The effects of culture or origin and permanence of relocation among international college students. *Journal of College Counseling, 3 (1),* 49–62.

Tabachnick, B. G., & Fidell, L. S. (2001). Using *multivariate statistics* (4th ed.). Boston, MA: Allyn & Bacon.

Thomas, R. M. (2003). *Blending qualitative and quantitative research methods in these and dissertations.* Thousand Oaks, CA: Corwin Press, Inc.

Thompson, B. R. (2004). *Exploratory and confirmatory factor analysis: Understanding concepts and applications.* Washington, DC: American Psychological Association.

Tinto, V. (1993). *Leaving college: Rethinking the causes and cures of student attrition.* Chicago: University of Chicago Press.

Tomich, P. C., McWhirter, J. J., & Darcy, M. U. (2003) Personality and international students' adaptation experience. *Journal of International Education, 33 (1)22-39.*

Toyokawa, T., & Toyokawa, N. (2002). Extracurricular activities and the adjustment of Asian international students: A study of Japanese students. *International Journal of Intercultural Relations, 26(4),* 363–379.

Toomey S. T., (1999). *Communicating Across Cultures.* New York, NY: Guilford Publications, Inc.

Triandis H. C., (2002). Individualism – collectivism and personality. *Journal of Personality, 69 (6),* 907–924.

Trompenaars, F., & Hampden-Turner, C. (1997). *Riding the waves of culture: Understanding cultural diversity in business.* London: Nicholas Brearley.

Trompenaars, F.,& Hampden-Turner, C. (1998). *Riding the waves of culture: Understanding cultural diversity in global business.* New York: McGraw-Hill.

Trow, M. (1989). American higher education – Past, present and future. *Studies in Higher Education, 14 (1),* 5–12.

Tseng, W., & Newton, F. B. (2002). International students' strategies for well-being. *College Student Journal, 36 (4),* 591–597.

Upcraft, M. L., Gardner, J. N., Barefoot, B. O., & Associates (2005). *Challenging & supporting the first year student: A handbook for improving the first year college.* San Francisco, CA: John Wiley & Sons, Inc.

Uekawa, K., Bowman K. M., & Lee, R. (2007). Student engagement in America's urban high school mathematics and science classrooms: Findings on social organization, race, and ethnicity. *The Urban Review, 39 (1),* 1–106.

Verbik, L. & Lasanowski, V. (2007). International student mobility: Patterns and trends, *The Observatory on Borderless Higher Education Report (OBHE).* Retrieved 12 December, 2009, from http://www.obhe.ac.uk

Voison, D. R., & Dillon-Remy, M. (2002). Psychocultural factors associated with HIV infection among Trinidad and Tobago adolescents. *Journal of HIV/AIDS Prevention & Education for Adolescents & Children 4 (2&3),* 65–82.

Volkan, V. D. (1999). Psychoanalysis and diplomacy: Part 1. Individual and large group identity. *Journal of Applied Psychoanalytic Studies, 1 (1), 29-55.*

Wade, C, & Travis, C. (2000). *Psychology* (6th ed.). Upper Saddle River, NJ: Prentice Hall Inc.

Wallen, N. E. & Fraenkel, J. R. (2001). Educational research: A guide to the process. Mahwah, New Jersey: Lawrence Erlbaum Associates.

Wan, T., Chapman, D. W., & Biggs, D. A. (1992). Academic stress of international students attending US universities. *Research in Higher Education, 33* (5), 607–622.

Wang, J., & Frank, D. G. (2002). Cross-cultural communication: Implications for effective information services in academic libraries. *Libraries and the Academy, 2,* 207–216.

Wang, C. C. & Mallinckrodt, B. (2006). Acculturation, attachment, and psychosocial adjustment of Chinese/Taiwanese international students. *Journal of Counseling Psychology. 53 (4),* 422–433.

Ward, C., Bochner, S., & Furnham, A. (2001). The *psychology of culture shock* (2nd ed.) East Sussex, England: Routledge.

Ward, C. & Kennedy, A. (2001). Coping with cross-cultural transition. *Journal of Cross-Cultural Psychology, 32 (5),* 636–42.

Ward, C. & Ran-Deuba, A. (1999). Acculturation and adaptation revisited. *Journal of Cross-Cultural Psychology, 30 (4),* 422–42.

Wartman, K.L & Savage, M. (2008). Parental involvement in higher education: Understanding the relationship among students, parents, and the institution. *ASHE Higher Education Report, 33(6),* 1-125.

Wintre, M.G., & Yaffe, M. (2000). First-year students' adjustment to university life as a function of relationships with parents. *Journal of Adolescent Research, 15 (1),* 9–37.

World Education Services (2007). Retrieved on January 22, 2010 at http://www.wes.org/eudcuators/pdf/StudentMobility.pdf World Education News and Reviews.

Yi, J. K., Lin, J. G., & Kishimoto, Y. (2003). Utilization of counseling services by international students. *Journal of Instructional Psychology, 30 (4),* 333–342.

Yang, E., Wong, S.C., Hwang, M., & Heppner, M. J. (2002). Widening our global view: The development of career counseling services for international students. *Journal of Career Development, 28(3),* 203–213.

Yankelovich, D, (2005). *The chronicle of higher education, the review. 52 (14),* B.6.

Ying, Y., & Liese, L. H. (1994). Initial adjustment of Taiwanese students to the U.S.: The impact of post-arrival variables. *Journal of Cross-Cultural Psychology, 25 (4),* 466 – 477.

Zakaria, N. (2000). The effects of cross-cultural training on the acculturation process of a global workforce. *International Journal of Manpower, 21 (6),* 492–510.

Zeszotarski, P. (2003). Expectations and experiences of international students in an American community college in the context of globalization. Doctoral dissertation, University of California, Los Angeles. (AAT 3089019).

Zhang, N. (2000). Acculturation and counseling expectancies: Asian international students' attitudes toward seeking professional psychological help. Unpublished doctoral dissertation, Ball State University, Muncie, IN.

Appendices

Appendix A

Survey Instrument

Foreign-born Student Adjustment Survey

Introduction: This survey is to learn about your thoughts, feelings and experiences at the US community colleges and to find ways to improve foreign-born students' adjustment to American colleges. Therefore, your participation is very important to us. Keep in mind that this exercise is strictly voluntary and all information provided is confidential. Because your privacy will be fully protected, you are not required to write you names, phone numbers, e-mail address or even student ID. Survey is expected to take about 15 to 20 minutes to complete. No one but this researcher will have access to the completed surveys. The information obtained from the survey will be reported only as group data for completing the dissertation. Thank you for taking time to complete this survey. Please answer all questions to the best of your ability.

Item A: Please check the box that best applies to you.

	Strongly Disagree	Disagree	Neither agree nor disagree	Agree	Strongly Agree
1. I don't feel like myself in this country					
2. I am able to do well here what I used to do in my home country					
3. I miss home a lot.					
4. I feel like I am alone here.					

5. I do not feel safe in this country because of whom I am.					
6. I don't feel like going to the counselor's office for help even when I have problems.					
7. My people may think that I am mad or crazy if they see me going into the counselor's office for help.					
8. I don't always feel safe simply because I am away from home.					
9. I feel always unhappy with the American Culture (way of life).					

	Strongly Disagree	Disagree	Neither agree nor disagree	Agree	Strongly Agree
10. I feel very unhappy (sad) easily when my ways of life are not accepted.					
11. I do not feel okay here in college because people here have ways of life different from mine.					
12. I have problems with American's way of life because of the way I was brought up in my family.					

13. I always want things done according to my own way of life and those of my own people.					
14. I find it hard to trust other people's ways of life that are different from my own people's ways of life.					
15. I miss my home country's food a lot.					
16. I miss our way of dressing a lot too					
17. I always feel that my own people's ways of life are better than American people's ways of life.					
18. The weather is not good for me.					

	Strongly Disagree	Disagree	Neither agree nor disagree	Agree	Strongly Agree
19. I worry a lot about my family back home.					
20. I do not always feel safe simply because I am away from my family.					
21. I often feel that I have lost the ways of life of my family and other things we like in the family.					
22. I feel like talking to my family back home everyday					
23. I miss my family's support a lot in so many ways.					
24. Talking to my family on the phone will always make me feel better.					
25. Talking to my family on the phone will make me not feel being alone (lonely).					
26. I like talking to my family first before I do anything important here.					
27. Education and learning in class here are more difficult than the one in my country.					

	Strongly Disagree	Disagree	Neither agree nor disagree	Agree	Strongly Agree
28. I always work hard more in class to pass well in order to make my family happy because that is what my people do (or are known for).					
29. I put more time in classroom work and studies than in other things else so as to keep doing well.					
30. I feel that I am not doing very well in class works because of my English.					
31. I don't trust American people for social interactions and lasting friendship.					
32. This college does not have enough things that help students here as we have in my home country.					
33. Americans do not accept other people's ways of life.					

	Strongly Disagree	Disagree	Neither agree nor disagree	Agree	Strongly Agree
34. I feel that I am able to relate well (interact) with American students in this country.					
35. I like to relate only with people from my own area or home country because I feel comfortable doing that.					
36. What I have seen in my home country makes me not like to interact with teachers here.					

	Yes	No	Do not know
37. Do you plan to continue your studies in this college?			
38. Do you plan to return home after your studies at this college?			
39. Do you feel like dropping out of the community college			
40. Do you plan to enroll in a four-year college/university when you finish in this college?			
41. In general, are you satisfied with your life in this college?			

42. Given the opportunity to begin your study again, would you select this community college as you place of study?			
43. Given the opportunity to begin your study again, would you select the US as you place of study?			
44. Would you recommend the US to other students in your home country who plan to study abroad			

Please answer the following Questions:

Item B: Demographics

1. What is you Gender?   a. Male o b. Female o

2. How old are you?
a. 18-25 o b. 26-35 o c. 36-45 o d. 46-55 o e. 56- 65 o f. over 65 o

3. What is your marital status? a. Married o b. Single o c. Divorced O

4. What is your stage at the community college (enrollment status)?
a. Year one o b. Year two o c. Year two and over o

5. In what academic program are you? Please indicate

_____

6. What is your Background/Continent? Please indicate:

a. Europe ○   b. Africa ○   c. Latin America ○   d. Asia ○   e. Middle East ○

f. North America

7. What is your country of origin /nationality (for example: Indian)? Please specify

_____

8. Do you have family here in the United States?

a. Yes ○   b. No ○

Appendix B
Focus Group Interview Questions

Introductory Questions:
1. Tell me about yourself without mentioning your name?
2. How long have you been here in the United States? Do you have family here in the US?
3. How long have you been here at the community college? In which academic program are you? What is your stage/year in college?

Post-Migration/Transitional Questions:
4. Tell me, how did/do you feel after you left your home country to study here in the US? What were your feelings when you first arrived here?
5. Could you give me examples of the challenges you face in this country after you left your home country?
6. How do you think and feel as you try to settle down here in this country? Could you describe your thinking and feelings?

Key Questions:
7. What are your thoughts about your own people's ways of life and American people's ways of life? Do you think there are differences between those two ways of life? What would you tell me about them and why do you think that way?
8. Could you tell me the nature of some of the problems you have with American people's *ways of life*?
9. Do you think there is something you are missing at home? What are they?

10. Would you say that you feel at home here in the US just the way you would feel in your home country? Why or why not? Do you think everything is okay with you right now from the way you feel?
11. Why do you think or feel that way? What do you think we can do to make you feel better here?
12. Do you think American people understand your way of life? Why or why not?
13. How do you think and feel when American people don't understand your ways of life and how do you react to them when that happens?
14. Do you ever think about going for counseling? What would you tell me now can make you not go for counseling? Give me examples of those reasons?
15. Do you think that you miss your family? How much do you miss your family? Why do you think that way? Why do you think that you miss them a lot?
16. What relationship do you keep with your family back home since you came to this country? How often do you communicate with them? Why do you feel like talking to them? In what ways do you feel that talking to them helps you?

Outcome Questions (Interaction and Academics):

17. Do you relate well with Americans? Why or why not? What do you think make your relationship with the American people hard? Just feel free to mention them.
18. Can you think of any examples of how differences in *ways of life* might change the way you interact with Americans?

19. Thinking of the way you were raised in school back home, what would you consider your academic challenges? Do you see anything different and why do think it is so?
20. Could you give me examples of the problems you have in school, especially in your studies? Why do you think so?
21. Do you think or feel there is something special in the academic system back in your home country? Do you think there are any differences? What are those differences?

Wrap up Questions:

22. Do you plan to continue your studies here in the United States when you finish here at the community college? Why or why not?
23. Do you have anything more to add in response to any of the questions you were asked?

www.ingramcontent.com/pod-product-compliance
Lightning Source LLC
Chambersburg PA
CBHW020418010526
44118CB00010B/311